M000048103

The Psychoanalysis of Symptoms

Henry Kellerman, Ph.D.

The Psychoanalysis
of Symptoms

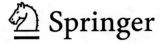 Springer

Henry Kellerman, Ph. D.
Postgraduate Center for Mental Health,
128 East 26 Street,
New York, NY 10016
USA
henrykellerman@earthlink.net

ISBN: 978-0-387-72247-4   e-ISBN: 978-0-387-72248-1

Library of Congress Control Number: 2007929735

© 2008 Springer Science+Business Media, LLC
All rights reserved. This work may not be translated or copied in whole or in part without the written per-
mission of the publisher (Springer Science+Business Media, LLC, 233 Spring Street, New York, NY
10013, USA), except for brief excerpts in connection with reviews or scholarly analysis. Use in
connection with any form of information storage and retrieval, electronic adaptation, computer software,
or by similar or dissimilar methodology now known or hereafter developed is forbidden.
The use in this publication of trade names, trademarks, service marks, and similar terms, even if they
are not identified as such, is not to be taken as an expression of opinion as to whether or not they are
subject to proprietary rights.

Printed on acid-free paper.

9 8 7 6 5 4 3 2 1

springer.com

To
our extraordinary
Sam Kellerman

Preface

Prevailing wisdom in the clinical arena has had it that each psychological symptom is a separate lock requiring its correspondingly unique key. Thus, it has been thought with respect to symptoms, that there are an infinite number of locks and a correspondingly infinite number of keys. Further, the psychoanalytic sense of it is that each symptom needs to be assessed, analyzed, and approached with reference to the unique experience of the patient and the patient's history; among other factors, also in terms of psychosexual conflict, and ego-strength. Given this position, it also has been felt that no single procedure, or code could be developed to address all symptoms of all patients as though, as an analogy, one lock and one key could apply to every symptom.

In this sense, there has been scarcely any attempt to derive a universal code that would address all symptoms with respect to the formation and structure of the symptom, regardless of the patient's particular experience and psychological history. In this volume, however, with only a few qualifications, I will present a single universal code to unlock any and all specifically defined psychological symptoms. I will present a system and procedure–a blueprint–with which to do it. One key.

Further, this procedure will be guided entirely by a set of propositions and axioms regarding each step in the unlocking of *any symptom*. The only qualifying conditions to this promise of presenting such a universal key for the unlocking of "any symptom," are these:

1. The symptom has not entirely radiated the person in terms of a psychotically deeply engraved pathology, which can best or even only be alleviated with medication.
2. The symptom has not been characteristic of the person for the major part of that person's life. It is not, in other words a chronic condition.
3. The symptom is not a chronically entrenched somatized one.
4. The symptom is not a function of a physiological problem, an organic brain syndrome, or genetic anomaly.
5. The symptom is not one of recent onset due to extreme trauma and based upon a profound sense of helplessness regarding the trauma, in which an implosion

of rage, unconscious though it may have been, has been chaotically scattered as rage-debris throughout the psyche.

6. The symptom is not a function of a less than normally resilient ego that would in turn generate a thin stimulus-barrier ultimately resulting in an exaggerated response to untoward or intense stimuli.

Other than such encrusted, overly ego-susceptible, somatically or organically based, and deeply etched pathological symptoms, all others are subject to an unlocking by this one master key.

That there are two classes of symptoms is clinically evident. The class of symptoms not easily treated, and quite resistant to psychotherapy, are those that swallow the person whole so that he or she, in a sense becomes the symptom. In contrast, the class of symptoms that indeed, is more easily subject to psychotherapy includes those that remain only as an aspect, an alien facet of the personality–seemingly outside of the personality.

Alleviation of emotional-psychological symptoms and symptom-cure is what we want to do. I have long believed that what psychoanalysts and psychotherapists accomplish has nothing to do with cure. The notion of cure regarding the psychoanalytic or psychotherapeutic endeavor misses the point. Life cannot be cured. The best we can do is to offer the patient the ability to develop tools with which to struggle, and to struggle better. No more, no less.

However, the only cure we do achieve, is with symptoms. This, despite the fact that there is no legacy either from Freud or anyone else that details a specific procedure or blueprint that we can use to proceed, in order to cure those symptoms that are subject to the talking cure in the same manner, and from a specific knowledge base, so that no matter the symptom, we can apply this template, penetrate the symptom, and cure it.

In this volume, as I've stated, a blueprint will be presented that forms the equation necessary to indeed penetrate the symptom and erase it, dissolve it, and cure it–eliminate it forever.

Organization of the Volume

In Part I, "Theoretical Context," the theoretical, scientific, and clinical literature on symptoms, their formation, and structure are considered. In addition, the symptom-code herein proposed, is presented with respect to its underpinnings, application, and relation to issues of personality.

In Part II, "The Clinical Casebook: Accessible Symptoms," examples of the class of symptoms are presented that can be understood, penetrated, and erased through the application of the symptom-code and by the talking cure–by psychotherapy. Such symptoms exist quite apart from the rest of the personality and are usually, but not always, of recent onset.

In Part III, "The Clinical Casebook: Inaccessible Symptoms," a variety of symptoms are presented that can be understood, but which cannot be easily penetrated or erased through the application of the symptom-code and psychother-apy. These are inaccessible symptoms of long standing, which have infiltrated the personality in such a way that the symptom and the person have become indistin-guishable. Furthermore, as stated, these inaccessible resistive symptoms are those of organic or genetic origin, or of a chronic somatization, or can reflect a psychot-ically chronic existence. In addition, as a result of an acute unconscious dispersion of rage-implosion, usually because of a profound trauma, the symptom may have been so infused into the fabric of the person's psyche, that the person's subjective experience would make elimination of such a symptom feel tantamount to elimi-nation of the personality itself. This also includes symptoms that are developed because of an absence of sufficient ego-resilience in the subject, making for a particularly exaggerated response to intense stimuli.

In Part IV, "Examining Theoretical Issues of the Symptom-Code," various issues are discussed in the treatment of symptoms that need further elaboration, research, theory, and synthesis, with an eye toward targeting those areas in the symptom arena that lack sufficient understanding. This sort of discussion is necessary because it should not be assumed that the arena of symptom cure, or even symptom understanding, is to date, complete. Save for the symptom-code presented in this volume, a systematic, ubiquitous approach to the penetration of the symptom has not been presented in the psychological literature as a cohesive body of work. Rather, the theory of symptoms, and the theory of the treatment of symptoms, including that referenced in Freud's published work, is actually distributed throughout the entire psychological and psychoanalytic literature, but only in a fragmentary fashion.

In addition, since the symptom-code presented here is so new, it needs time to be tested by clinicians as they utilize it to approach the wide variety of symptoms presented to them by their patients. Along with this need for more scholarly and clinical work regarding symptom cure, the class of symptoms labeled here as "inaccessible" has not been codified or attacked with any theoretical system that would tie various propositions together regarding such symptoms, in any useful nomological network. Finally, there still does not exist any formulation that syn-thesizes a general theory for the cure of symptoms here defined as "accessible" along with those defined as "inaccessible."

Thus, these four parts of this work will set forth:

1. What has been accomplished to the present, with respect to the scientific and clinical literature on the understanding of symptom formation and symptom cure;
2. The formulation of a new symptom-code which, when applied, claims the power of understanding, penetrating, and curing those symptoms that are of relatively recent duration, and not radiated the psyche by a colossal imploded rage due to some profound, intractable trauma;
3. The explication of a class of symptoms that can be considered inaccessible and therefore resistive to cure by the talking method, along with an analysis of the infrastructure of such symptoms, revealing the essential problem of their treatment;

4. A presentation of theoretical issues detailing the outlines of the entire symptom
domain so that what needs to be done with respect to clinical formulation for a
more comprehensive synthesis of the field, can perhaps be more clearly visible.

It has been more than a decade since I began to formulate the various assumptions and propositions that together enabled the crystallization of the series of
axioms to be presented. The entire system is explicated here along with a number
of clinical cases of a wide variety of symptoms, showing how the cure is effected.

Over this past decade I have been teaching the code for symptom cure to
postdoctoral students and professional clinicians, as well as utilizing the symptom-code in the supervision of cases In this present volume I am able to present
the ideas and terms of the symptom-code more comprehensively, bringing to bear
on the subject matter, the relevant psychological literature, and spelling out
symptom cure in technical, systematic, clinical, and scientific terms.

The accessible symptoms referred to throughout this volume are the emo-
tional/psychological one's patients bring to treatment. They are endless in variety
and sometimes can seem weird, bizarre, often exasperating, and to the patient,
usually embarrassing. These symptoms, subject to psychotherapy, all have at least
two things in common: one, they are experienced by the person as something
strange, even alien; and two, they can all be cured using the same method. *One*
key for *all* the locks.

I believe that once patients begin to work with this master key, they themselves
will be able to help the therapist help them. It is hoped that the confusing,
symbolic, other-worldly nature of symptoms will become much more responsive
to the psychotherapeutic touch as a result of therapists and patients, working
together to quickly unlock the symptom. *Quickly* is the operative term here;
because to do it quickly is important in that it can sometimes take years before the
symptom is cured. And frequently symptoms get cured, not because we necessarily knew how we did it, or even knew how it came about. Rather, because of the
multitude of interactional permutations occurring, sometimes over a period of
years, ultimately, the symptom is dissolved perhaps because of the efficacy of
interpretation, and generally, perhaps because of the overall therapeutic work that
was accomplished. Other than that, we indeed see symptom cure from time to
time, simply by the patient's flight into health, or by the patient's acute positive
transference. Nevertheless, these can be considered inadvertent symptom cures, a
side-effect of other variables, and not cures that are the result of a specific knowledge base that the therapist possesses, or the use of a specific procedure that the
therapist systematically implements to accomplish the aim of helping patients
dissolve symptoms.

In formulating the code that reflects the entire blueprint of this symptom curing
procedure, as well as its underlying assumptions and propositions, I have had to
offer alternate equations that recalibrate some basic Freudian precepts. In this
present work it should also be noted that historical and transferential issues that
arise as a result of the process of symptom cure can then be further pursued in the
ongoing unfolding of the patient's psychotherapy.

I believe it needs to be remembered that a useful theory is one that works best empirically. Framing it in more universal scientific terms, the most useful, or most powerful theory, is the one that can explain the widest array of phenomena with respect to the fewest number of variables.

One master key.

Table of Contents

Part I
Theoretical Context

Chapter 1
History of Symptom Psychology

The history of psychological symptom formation as a clinical and scientific subject of interest, is of course, tied to the work of Sigmund Freud. Most of the elements of the entire anatomy of what is considered a symptom–its constituents, structure, and its very foundation–is considered throughout Freud's collected works, although actually in a fragmentary fashion, located in just about all of his work, either directly or by implication. From his 1894 paper on the defence neuropsychoses (1894/1962), to the Fragment of an Analysis of a Case of Hysteria, 1905/1953), to his papers on Inhibition, Symptoms, and Anxiety, 1926/1959), wherever one looks, it seems that everything ultimately points toward symptom as psychopathology. Thus, just about all of Freud's work, in one way or another, can be correlated to almost every facet of the subject of symptoms.

A cursory listing of some of the considerations Freud raised, either having direct relevance to the study of symptoms, or implying important issues in this study, can easily comprise a separate glossary of Freudian terms and concepts. The following is only an illustrative sample of this sort of compendium.

Conflict between ego and id; the function of defenses; the special nature of repression; equilibrium of drives; consciousness versus the unconscious; compromise formations; drive derivatives and fear and guilt; breakthrough of drives; analogy to a manifest dream; similarity of dreams and symptoms; substitute gratifications; repressed wishes; pleasure and unpleasure; ego alien material; anxiety; symptoms as a way of removing the ego from danger; instinctual demand; primary and secondary gain; overdetermindness; helplessness; unbearable ideas; conversion; symptom precipitators–grief, despair, depression; sexual wishes and repression; recathexis of object representation; narcissistic satisfaction; castration fear; energy fortification.

Thus, in Freud's amalgam of variables bearing on the appearance of symptoms, their source, purpose, formation, and structure, the above listing is really only a modest sample of the massive amount of theoretical and clinical material that Freud brought to bear on the study of symptoms and their treatment.

In distilling the essence of his position and particular understanding of symptoms, he proposed that a symptom is part of a solution to a situation that the person deems to be dangerous. Of course, Freud's position is that such danger originates from the person's own impulses. In his "Fragment of an Analysis of a

Case of Hysteria" (1905/1953), he indicated that in the process of the solution to this dangerous situation, the symptom will form, thus necessarily producing an impairment of a usual function. In "Inhibition, Symptoms and Anxiety," (1926/1959) he stated that then a new phenomenon will appear that has arisen out of this impairment. This process, he continued, ends in the symptom that has removed the ego from danger, an end result that has also disguised the person's wish (a forbidden wish) as the symptom. It is the conflict between these forbidden, (usually sexual) wishes, and corresponding repressive forces, that then, according to Freud, underlies every neurotic or psychological symptom. In fact, according to Freud, all symptoms are derived from childhood sexual disturbance.

Finally, with respect to Freud's salient dimensions of symptoms and symptom formation, the concept of repression needs to be emphasized. Freud (1936/1961), stated that: "A symptom arises from an instinctual impulse which has been detrimentally affected by repression" (p. 8). The forbidden nature of the impulse that invites repression, concerns the threat of punishment, the agency of which Freud initially proposed, was castration anxiety. Repression also needs constant energy fortification. So, because instincts are continuous, the ego must provide a permanent expenditure of energy to keep these instincts repressed. Then, ultimately, the manifestation and dynamic operation of the phenomenon of resistance, is what is generated to protect this repression.

This idea of the use of resistance to protect repression also establishes the psychoanalytic definition of acting out, distinguishing this psychoanalytic definition from that of psychiatry. The psychiatric focus regarding acting out concerns the behavior of the subject; that is, the person in action. In contrast, the psychoanalytic focus of acting out is not primarily about behavior so much as it is about the attempt the subject makes *not to know something*. Freud's observation and discovery was that repression is what keeps the person from being conscious of concealed, dangerous impulses or thoughts that he or she is harboring. Further, Freud's profound insight with respect to this issue of repression was that the patient's resistance assured the sustaining of the repression. Therefore, rather than knowing or seeing these impulses or thoughts, the person behaves in ways that motorically symbolize the repressed material. It is in this sense that acting out, in the context of human history, may be the first ubiquitous symptom–*doing, rather than knowing*–the quintessential psychoanalytic definition of acting out.

Freud, in other words, posits that a compromise takes place that neutralizes the danger of a sexual impulse (the instinct), but then causes the impairment of a usual function, and in its place there arises the formation of a new phenomenon, the symptom. Again, the ego is thus removed from danger and the wish becomes actually gratified as a transformed entity, the symptom. This is an important point, a discovery of major proportion; to wit, that the symptom is really the wish realized, albeit in neurotic or perverse form.

This insight of the relationship between the wish and the symptom leads us inexorably to Freud's definitive axiom regarding wishes and repression, one that has the unmistakable ring of psychoanalytic truth; that is, *no wish will be denied.* It may be that the psyche is so pervasively governed, so wired, and even fueled by the pleasure principle, that this self-same psyche regards the wish as an imperative, and as such, does an undeniable, almost mathematical dance, a contortion of sorts, to get the wish represented, gratified– in the extreme form of a seemingly incomprehensible symptom.

Other Authors

Many other authors have considered symptoms in general terms, restated Freud's psychoanalytic position regarding the etiology of symptoms, attempted to further understand the structure of the symptom, or suggested ways of elucidating various specific facets of the symptom or of its formation (Alexander, 1950; Arlow, 1969; Brenner, 1973; Deutsch, 1953; Fenichel, 1945; Greenacre, 1958; Josephs, 1992; Kellerman, 1987; Luborsky, 1996; Rangell, 1959; and Seligman, 1975).

Brenner (1973) validated Freud by pointing to the importance of defense as a way of keeping an equilibrium in the psyche. This equilibrium acts as an ego adaptation to the stress of the drives. The symptom, therefore, is seen to be a result of a failure of ego defenses. Brenner wrote that as the conflict between the ego and id intensifies, defenses of identification, regression, and sublimation, are utilized to further control the drives. Yet, when drives threaten to break through–to emerge into consciousness–and correspondingly, when defenses are deemed insufficient to sustain an equilibrium of the psyche, the ego then struggles to create a compromise. This compromise, of course, is the psychoneurotic symptom. Brenner further concurred with Freud by noticing the similarity of the symptom to the manifest dream; that is, the descriptive story line of the dream. As such, and just as in a dream, a wish on the part of the subject is of primary importance in the momentum toward the formation of the actual dream, just as the wish is of primary importance in the formation of the symptom. In order to be understood, the manifest dream must be unfolded into its latent products through an analysis of the dream mechanisms of condensation, symbolization, displacement, and secondary elaboration. So too, is the implication that the symptom needs to be unfolded by a process that utilizes mechanisms that have psychologically evolved to address the intrinsic structure of the symptom. For example, in the dream, these dream mechanisms are considered to do the following: two or more elements are condensed into one, hence condensation; one thing can represent another, hence symbolization; one thing can be transposed to another, hence displacement; and, elaborations can be made that coalesce the various and sundry sense impressions, images, thoughts, and feelings, into a more coherent story, hence secondary elaboration.

The Freudian notion of the parallel between the manifest dream and the psychoneurotic symptom begs to be compared in the same manner. What are the mechanisms that are brought to bear on the Freudian precept of the ego-id conflict where the person's psychological experience was incubated in the first place, resulting in the appearance of the symptom? The question arises as to whether such symptom mechanisms may be identified and defined so that an X ray of the symptom as constituted, showing its structure, the location of the wish, how the wish is transformed into the symptom, and so on, could be developed. This would comprise an analysis of the infrastructure of the symptom, and, in essence, would constitute the psychoanalysis of symptoms.

Identifying the wish is of central importance with respect to this X ray of the psyche. Brenner (1973), stated:

As seen from the side of the id, a psychoneurotic symptom is a substitute gratification for otherwise repressed wishes. As seen from the side of the ego, it is an eruption into consciousness of dangerous and unwanted wishes whose gratification can be only partly checked or prevented, but it is at least preferable to, and less pleasurable than, the emergence of those wishes in their original form. (p. 189).

In this sense, thus far in the theoretical investigation of the structure of the symptom, we can see that the wish, defense mechanisms, and instinctual drives form a primary Freudian focus in understanding how the symptom is formed. Then, by way of extrapolation, we may wonder whether it would be possible, through a series of axioms, to know how to systematically unravel the symptom, dissolve it, or, even hold it in abeyance, so that we may reconstitute the original wish that the symptom is ostensibly representing as well as concealing. In doing this unraveling, the issue of anxiety as it relates to symptom formation needs to be examined. In addition, it is proposed here that the assumption of repressed wishes as unpleasurable products of the psyche may need to be reexamined.

Anxiety

It should be remembered that from a Freudian psychoanalytic perspective (Freud, 1905/1953), the symptom derives from a series of events, a process, that is taking place outside of the ego, so that in its formation, the symptom removes the ego from danger. Freud posited that the ego becomes more and more helpless in the face of increasing instinctual demand. A point to be discussed later concerns the issue of anxiety itself as a symptom and what this implies. Regarding the importance or place of anxiety in symptom formation, Luborsky (1996) stated that anxiety is the original reaction to helplessness. The symptom then becomes the first way to cope with this helplessness.

The entire issue of helplessness and anxiety, is of special importance in understanding symptom formation, and Luborsky's reference to it permits us to include issues of helplessness and anxiety to the expanding list of salient concepts that will need even further elaboration to enable us to penetrate the symptom. Such a list would now include: the wish; defense mechanisms; instinctual drives; anxiety; and, helplessness. In fact, Luborsky stated: "Wherever symptoms appear, helplessness appears before it; whenever helplessness has appeared, symptoms occasionally follow it" (p. 370). Luborsky also stated: . . . . ."after the symptom appears degree of helplessness and of anxiety lessens."

As proposed, and whether intended or not, Luborsky's formulations are basically framed as axioms. Luborsky continued to assess the relationship between anxiety and symptoms by positing that with the symptom present, anxiety is better bound and thus yields a primary gain for the subject. The subject, however, also attracts help from others and thereby creates a secondary gain. The case is also made by Luborsky that, "signal anxiety exists before the symptom appears in an amount just sufficient to announce that a danger situation is about to appear" (p.369). On the face of it, it would also seem that anxiety and helplessness are related, and that they are related in the overall puzzle of symptom formation and possibly by implication, symptom cure.

The helplessness variable is also referred to by Engel and Schmale (1967), who point to what they call a "giving-up/given-up" complex. This is a nonspecific presymptomatic state. It contains a cluster of tendencies and characteristics including: a lessening of control and a lessening of a sense of security, helplessness and hopelessness, less certainty of one's perceptions of the environment and of past experience, and a clouding of differentiation between past and future. Seligman (1975), concurred, insofar as negative events lead to pessimism in the subject and then to vulnerability to symptoms, especially to the increase of depression. Seligman called it "learned helplessness." The extreme form of such helplessness is posited in an early book by Goldstein (1939), who discussed catastrophic behavior as a prelude to substitute reactions such as symptoms.

Repression and the Hint of a Key Emotion in Symptom Formation

With respect to conversion reactions (conventionally referred to as hysterical reactions or hysteria), Freud (1894/1962) proposed that in hysteria, the unbearable idea is obscured and minimized by the amount of excitation attached to it, and then the idea is translated into some bodily language, or bodily form of expression. Freud called this process, conversion. Fenichel (1945) also referred to conversions. He indicated that the turning of reality to fantasy was a precursor to conversions. Here again, repression seems to play a key role insofar as the turning of reality into fantasy constitutes a withdrawal and implies a repressive process at work, necessary in the formation of a symptom.

Parenthetically, this turning away from reality also suggests that the individual was unable to directly or consciously confront some forbidden wish or emotion. If it was an emotion that was avoided, which one was it? Further, which emotion is most frequently avoided, and avoided specifically with respect to confrontation? Is it always, or usually, some sexual reference as Freud might have proposed? Is it anxiety? So far as symptom formation is concerned, it will be proposed here that Freud's sexual repression is only an *apparent* culprit implicated in the understanding of the role of impulse and instinct on the one hand, and repression on the other. However, where repression is concerned, it will be further proposed that an emotion or instinct, other than sexual, is the *actual* culprit.

We cannot guess what any given wish in any person might be, because there may be an indeterminate number of literal or concrete wishes in humanity's psyche. Thus, there is probably not a universal wish that could be identified as pivotal in all symptom formation. With respect to emotion, however, there are only a limited number of basic emotions that might be implicated in all symptom formation–an emotion other than sexuality–that may be the actual culprit. Assuming this as a possibility, is that emotion love, fear, acceptance, disgust, guilt, anger, joy, anxiety, or sorrow? In this volume I shall identify which it is: One thing is quite certain–it is not sexuality or libido–repressed or not.

The Idea of Constant Terms

The point here is that constant terms exist in the symptom equation, the application of which, I propose, will lead to the unfolding of the symptom. It is hypothesized that there is, in this particular conception, one primary emotion that is identified as a constant term in this equation. In Freud's view, the ubiquitous wish is another such constant. Freud proposed that conversion is employed to express forbidden wishes (sexual), which again, in his view, is the true purpose of all symptoms. And the essence of conversion consists of displacing energy from the psyche to the body. In this sense, the derivatives of forbidden impulses are expressed in a distorted manner–in other words, in the manner of symptoms. The symptom, then can be considered a distorted product of the psyche. There are many synonyms of "distorted," at least two of which are immediately apparent: *neurotic*, and *perverse*.

The attempts at various theoretical refinements of what has been understood as the underpinning to symptom formation cited by authors referred to above, can also apply to the proposal by Luborsky (1964, 1996), in his symptom context method. Luborsky studied what he refers to as symptoms such as forgetting, that occur during any given single psychoanalytic session. Momentary forgetting during a session is seen by Luborsky to be the result of a particular thought about which the person feels anxious and helpless. A symptom then appears to help a person cope with these uncomfortable feelings. Ferenczi (1912/1950), was also interested in symptoms that occurred during a session and analyzed what he called "transient symptoms."

Both Ferenczi and Luborsky wanted to understand the context in which the symptom occurs–in Luborsky's case, the forgetting during a session. The question becomes whether the forgetting is actually a symptom. A tentative answer might be that in Luborsky's view of symptoms, if the forgetting is not remediable, then a symptom appeared primarily because the patient was *helpless* to recall the memory or thought. The helplessness then promoted a chain of events leading to the defeat of the effort to consciously capture the wish; that is, to recall the thought. However, if the patient is still trying to recall whatever it is, so that the wish is not relinquished and therefore helplessness has still not gained the ascendancy, then the promotion of that chain of events culminating in a symptom, would not be joined.

In this respect, with regard to the wish and helplessness, in the following I will suggest a new way of understanding the psychoanalysis of symptoms and ultimately to present a complement of axioms and clinical cases where these rules are followed. This system will demonstrate that where applied, the use of these axioms can lead to the efficient dissolution of the symptom–its cure.

Chapter 2
Underpinnings of the Symptom Code

Themes

The capsule review in the previous chapter of the psychoanalytic concepts involved in symptom formation reveals several components in the construction and organization of symptoms that will now be further considered. The focus here will be to present a series of axioms or rules regarding the symptom and the various psychological principles embracing it, so that in the end, by understanding these principles, and by utilizing the rules or axioms, a practitioner would be able to systematically penetrate the conundrum of the symptom, unfold it, and cure it.

Of course, the psychoanalytic endeavor generally, is not about cure, it is only, as noted in the Preface, about struggle. The only curing we do however, is the curing of symptoms, despite the fact that no one has ever established any systematic way of doing it. In fact, there is an absence of any systematic approach to understanding symptoms, as for example, in the absence of any course work either in undergraduate, graduate, or even postgraduate curricula entitled "The Psychoanalysis of Symptoms," or "The Psychology of Symptoms." The issue of symptoms is usually a secondary consideration in courses on psychopathology, or abnormal psychology. Furthermore, the nature of our theoretical repository sources regarding an approach to symptom cure is similarly quite fragmentary. It seems that the symptom is seen as derivative of something else, and in psychoanalytic education is given secondary status to a focus on the patient's psychosexual history, transference, resistance, neurosis, and characterological issues, that are of primary psychoanalytic interest. This, despite the vast amount of material on symptoms throughout Freud's written work, as well as a considerable literature on symptoms within psychological, psychoanalytic, and psychiatric scholarship. It is in this sense that the focus in psychoanalysis is on process and not specifically on cure.

As noted above, through psychoanalysis, people learn to struggle better. There is no such thing as eliminating anxiety. It is the pleasure principle that governs, so anxiety becomes a fact of life. The pleasure principle is the fount from which every symptom is derived. The wish for the complete absence of tension defines both the pleasure principle and the death instinct. As a matter of fact, Freud's notion of a death instinct is primarily based upon the inexorable desire to erase tension. Thus, with respect to both the pleasure principle and the so-called death instinct, the symptom becomes a means to manage the presence of tension–albeit neurotically expressed tension. In addition, the wish is the steady-state product of the pleasure principle, and reflects its stasis. In daily life, it is the *wish* that is most often thwarted. Thus, it is a look at the thwarted wish–this ever present force in all human affairs, that begins our journey into the heart of the symptom.

Luborsky (1996), is correct, each symptom, no matter how simple, complex, or seemingly bizarre, has a context. It is proposed here that it is necessary to consider both the context as well as the source of the symptom in order to begin to understand the underpinnings of the problem. The problem, of course, concerns the etiology of the symptom as it relates to symptom cure. In fact, it is proposed here that the order of importance, chronologically, in the etiology of the symptom, needs to consider source first, then context.

The source is the pleasure principle, and its chief representative in all human desire and human affairs is *the wish*. It is the wish that is at the bottom of all symptom formation. However, before the wish is considered, it is necessary to define what we mean by a symptom.

Defining the Symptom

Here, of course, we are concerned with an emotional-psychological symptom: "emotional," because a major specific emotion is involved in all symptom formation; "psychological," because a dynamic involving defensive operations such as resistance, and specifically, repression, act to enable the existence of the symptom, and in addition, the same mechanisms that operate in dream formation—symbolization, condensation, and displacement–operate again, also in the process that enables the symptom to exist. Only the mechanism known as secondary elaboration is absent in the formation of the symptom. This is so because it is precisely the secondary elaboration–the logic and coherence to the original story–that the subject needed erased, and in fact, was erased by repression. In this way the subject remains in the dark about what it is that the symptom means. Thus, it could be said that with respect to analogy, the symptom can be located somewhere between the manifest and the latent dream.

There is no need for logic in the symptom. In this sense, the symptom has a certain kinship with, and is more similar to the latent dream–that amalgam, in the unconscious, of amorphous bombardment of stimuli, reflecting conflicts, fixations, and hungers. Along with this, the symptom is also similar to the manifest dream insofar as the wish is symbolically cohered into a tightly knit entity (the symptom) and is thus congealed, more like the manifest, and less like the latent dream.

Luborsky (1996) contributed to the understanding of the formation of symptoms, again, by insisting that the symptom has a context. However, both the immediate context in which the symptom is born, as well as the motive source of the symptom, need to be considered in order to develop a complete picture of the formation of the symptom and its meaning. In fact, in the order of importance, again chronologically, in the etiology of the symptom, the motive source of the symptom needs to be appreciated first, so as to make sense out of the meaning of the immediate context of the symptom. The source, of course, is the pleasure principle, and as stated, its chief representative in all human desire and human affairs, is *the wish*. It is the *wish* that is at the bottom of all symptom formation.

At least three elements comprise the definition of a symptom. All are ultimately experienced by the subject, so that these elements are existential.

1. A symptom is an *involuntary reaction* that the person experiences. This means that something happens that is outside the person's control–that can't at all be voluntarily controlled.
2. A symptom is an *ego-alien reaction*. This means that the symptom reaction feels different from anything else in the personality, as though it has been produced by a force outside of the personality–the person, feels possessed.
3. A symptom is a *tyrannical reaction* within the personality. This means, that whether the subject likes it or not, the symptom controls the subject and not the other way around.

Furthermore, a distinction needs to be made between those symptoms that can be cured through the talking method, and those that resist it. In the former, the emotion that is repressed remains cohered within the repression, and within the repression the image of the symptom context also remains intact. In other words, in the psyche, in the unconscious, the entire configuration of the symptom retains its integrity and becomes as aspect of the personality. In such a case, the key implicated emotion has not imploded, and thus this emotion has not strewn its debris throughout the psyche thereby infecting the entire personality with its radiating pathology.

The symptom that resists cure through the talking method is one in which the specific pathological emotion has indeed imploded, and the person's psyche, personality, character structure, chemistry, and nervous system, has been entirely permeated, thereby contaminating his or her inner psychological and emotional life in a way that can be considered a basic usurpation of the personality. It is further proposed, that in the unconscious, *the symptom that resists cure is also one in which the internalized image– the memory of the symptom context–is no longer in tact, and especially, no longer connected to the repressed emotion.*

In this sense, it will be predicted that because the connection of the stimulus (symptom context) to the specific and ubiquitous emotion that was repressed, becomes disconnected, that the symptom will no longer be merely an aspect or a facet of the personality. Rather, such a symptom swallows the personality, as it were, so that the symptom becomes the personality and not just an aspect of it. In this latter condition, the only seeming cure for the symptom is a longer term treatment and the likely use of medication. How and why this disconnect of the symptom context to the key repressed specific emotion causes such a catastrophic reaction will be discussed later.

To continue with this image of pathological debris infiltrating and permeating the person's entire inner life, a useful metaphor for what medications actually do might be to imagine that they begin to surround this so-called debris, and further, begin to collect, condense, congeal, and therefore contain it, until the person is free of contamination. Within this latter chronically encrusted and sometimes psychotic symptom condition, either with the ingestion of medicine along with a longer term treatment, the symptom will possibly abate.

In contrast, examples of symptoms that can be approached successfully through psychotherapy, are those that do not swallow the person whole. Such symptoms remain a part of the person that the person recognizes as troublesome or alien and outside of personal control, but which generally can be compartmentalized and at least managed, to some appreciable extent, even if not always adaptively. For example, if it is an acrophobic symptom, the person can avoid heights; if it is an agoraphobic symptom the person may be able to avoid crowds, or limit one's forays to the outside. One of the main points in defining the term *symptom,* is to understand that the symptom is the end result of a series of events that begins with the consideration of a wish.

The Wish

As the chief representative of the pleasure principle, the wish is the most pervasive, permeating force within the personality. The problem is that in life there are too many variables that are not within anyone's complete or sometimes, even partial control. The upshot of such meager control of wishes is that everyone's daily life is continually replete with thwarted wishes, sometimes big, sometimes small. If wishes are not fully thwarted, then they are perhaps only partially blocked. Or, whenever the wish is indeed realized, then frequently it is not realized to the fullest measure – and even when the wish is realized to the fullest measure, this frequently takes place not exactly when it is wanted. Thus, despite the fact that we are a wish-soaked species, on an earth of wish soaked-creatures, the irony is that wishes are usually in a state of incompleteness – their benign form, in a state of delay; in its severe form, in a deprived, fully thwarted state.

In addition, most people find it difficult to make distinctions between important and unimportant wishes. All wishes are treated as being more or less equally important – no less, and urgent. Apparently, there are no small wishes in the psyche. With many people, the slightest frustration of a wish – minor though the wish may be – creates the same disempowerment that the frustration of a major wish does. Hence, the thwarting of wishes in a person can be seen to occupy an inordinate amount of psychological concern.

On a practical level, the definition of civilized living, or of civilization itself, perhaps concerns the issue of how to survive, and survive happily, in the context of daily experience in which only simple wishes are really ever met with *efficiency;* for example, to turn on the hot water and have it be hot–wish gratified.

But to wish that your request for a substantial raise in salary will be *efficiently* met, can usually mean disappointment.

The Gratified Wish Means Empowerment

Wishes mean that one gets a wish gratified and achieves mastery, then the person feels empowered. When the wish is thwarted then the person is disappointed and feels disempowered, or as Freud (1926/1959), Luborsky (1996), and Seligman, (1975) noted, feels helpless. Apparently, in the psychological literature, and for all intents and purposes, *helplessness* and *disempowerment* are terms that may be used interchangeably.

Thus, because wishes are in such profusion, and because such wishes are most frequently thwarted, then the issue of disempowerment becomes essential in the understanding of the connection of wish to symptom. Here again, it is important to remember Freud's brilliant insight; that is, *no wish will be denied*. This insight was based upon Freud's proposition that dreams are wish fulfillments (Freud, 1900/1953a, pp.122–133). Arlow and Brenner (1964), indicate that Freud's proposition refers to unconscious wishes. Thus, we now necessarily know that in order for the wish not to be denied, something psychological has to happen; that is, in the face of reality where most wishes are in fact denied, then some psychological mechanism will need to be applied so that the wish will not be denied. And according to Freud, this psychological mechanism is repression-a force exerted on the effect of the thwarted wish, so that ultimately the symptom will appear. The symptom will be the wish in a new form, albeit a neurotic, or perverse one.

In this sense of concealing the effect or emotional reaction to the thwarted wish, repression is implicated, and becomes indispensable to the process of translating the wish into the symptom. Repression emerges as a chief defensive function because it is able to distort, distract, and otherwise dislocate the presumed instinctual impulse, and in this way, any threat of punishment for having such impulses is out of awareness and thus neutralized. Of course, in the history of psychoanalysis, this instinctual impulse is usually defined as libido.

Typical psychoanalytic understanding of this issue of repression of the wish (the sexual impulse), as a foundation of the formation of the symptom, is a conventional Freudian postulate. Suffice it to say, the important issue here concerns whether the pivotal repression involving wishes and symptoms, always or even *ever*, specifically involves repression of sexual impulses. Of course such a question becomes heretical; is it the sexual repression or is it the issue of the thwarted wish and what the thwarted wish produces–its emotional product–that becomes crucial in the evocation of the defense of repression that then leads to the subsequent ignition of the symptom? Is a sexual impulse always or even eve*r*, the result of a thwarted wish? This is a crucial question because when the wish is thwarted, no one is really ever happy. When the wish is thwarted, everyone is distressed, disturbed, disappointed, and dissatisfied. And this seemingly logical conclusion of thwarted wishes producing distress, perhaps reveals what might be considered the *actual* emotional culprit in the formation of symptoms. That is to say, *when the wish is thwarted, the person is angry.* This raises the second question that asks: Given the assumption that everyone is angry because of thwarted wishes, then *why* is everyone angry at thwarted wishes?

Anger

The answer to this question regarding the experience of anger to thwarted wishes, is that thwarted wishes generate feelings of disempowerment, of helplessness. Thus, it is evident one might say, on the face of it, that even in the thwarting of sexual wishes (sexual impulses), disempowerment and anger will be evoked. And to Freud's axiom that no wish will be denied, we add an axiom of our own: *Anger, or anger as a sample emotion of the aggressive drive, is the emotional reflex that has evolved in evolution to address each and every incident of disempowerment.*

The rationale for this axiom concerns the natural equilibrium all people seek. This equilibrium concerns the issue of mastery over the immediate environment. We want to be empowered! It feels good. Thus, when we feel disempowered, we get angry. The question is why?

Anger is an attack emotion, and by nature, it is not shy. The essence, or we might say, the personality of anger can be understood by the presence of a cluster of traits that characterize its nature-a kind of personality profile of anger consisting of an *attack* proclivity, *an explosive* potential, *an aggressive* drive, *a confrontational inclination, and* an *entitled frame of mind.* Furthermore, and parenthetically, these traits are all reactions to feelings of disempowerment, helplessness, or even dependency. Of course, dependency is a special form of disempowerment or helplessness. For example, adolescent rebellion after all those years of dependency, makes more sense when seen through this particular lens of dependency incubating anger. Clinically, the hard-core psychological principle is that dependency breeds rage–all the time and in every person. Disempowerment and helplessness also breed rage, which is the high intensity level of anger. And here is the logic and answer to why disempowerment generates anger: *To feel angry is to regain the ascendancy and to feel empowered when one feels particularly disempowered. And at times when there is no other way to find some empowerment, anger will be the reflex in response to the disempowered condition because for that moment it will be the only way to feel, at least minimally, reempowered.*

Yes, anger is an empowerment, and this brings us back to the wish. In light of the psychology of disempowerment leading to anger, the implication for a theoretical gradient of anger reaction, reveals itself. For example, even though in the psyche all wishes are major, nevertheless, there exists an implicit "thwarting-index" so that when a person's wish is thwarted a little, then the person, in all likelihood, generates a low level of anger, perhaps at the level of annoyance. When the thwarted wish is experienced as moderate, then it could be predicted that the person will generate a medium level of anger. However, when the wish is very important to the person and then subsequently thwarted, the anger will be more intense and will, in all probability, be generated as rage or fury–sometimes conscious, sometimes not.

In a practical sense, the problem that emerges here concerns this psychological phenomenon regarding the insignificant extent to which people distinguish between major and minor wishes. The interesting psychological fact, of course, is that most people do not distinguish between major and minor wishes so that, in effect, every wish becomes important. "I want what I want when I want it," is then the operative condition, a result that implicates emotions of anger and rage as most commonplace in everyday life.

With so many people trying to manage such a great amount of disappointment, dissatisfaction, and disempowerment to thwarted wishes, and then reacting with a corresponding ratio of anger and rage to such disempowerment, it is no wonder that the lexicon for anger comprises the largest glossary of terms, in contrast to any other emotion in the human emotion dictionary. For example, the general terms of *stress* or *anxiety* and their wider and deeper meaning can be illuminated if such terms are understood to be oblique references to suppressed or repressed anger at conditions that place the person under pressure so that satisfaction of wishes becomes unlikely, or probably unlikely, or just out of reach, or too much to hope for. The earlier issue regarding anxiety as a possible symptom itself, may now suggest that anxiety could actually be a radiating effect of what is below–repressed anger! Thus, the lexicon for anger can contain terms such as *upset*, or even *bored*. *Upset* is more easily understood; when something is really upsetting, is the person happy? No, the person is angry but doesn't want to face it. When someone is bored, she or he feels trapped in a tedious situation, but because it may not be socially desirable to be angry in such a situation, the conscious reaction is to only feel bored.

So which is the road to the repressive process leading to the formation of the symptom–the sexual frustration, that is to say, pent-up libido, or the anger regarding disempowerment? Which is the culprit – sex or anger? They're not the same. The answer is surprising, given the century-old reliance on the psychoanalytic precept of sexual repression as more or less, the insidious and pervasive culprit in symptom formation, and for all intents and purposes, in all of psychopathology as well.

The resounding answer is: *Anger is the culprit*. More specifically, repressed anger is the culprit. In order for there to be a symptom, the anger must be repressed. Freud was the first to enunciate the general principle regarding this process of repression, and just about all other theoreticians have echoed that insight or discovery. The discovery, the general principle, was that in order for there to be a symptom, a repression of the instinctual impulse, understood to the present time to be sexual repression, was the constant in the theoretical understanding of symptom formation.

Theoretically, repression was always indispensable to the process of how the wish transforms into the symptom. The question raised here is only about whether the instinctual impulse is sex or anger. Nevertheless, repression emerges as a chief defensive function in this transformation of the wish to the symptom. This is so because, as stated earlier, according to accepted psychoanalytic understanding, repression is able to redirect the instinctual impulse thus neutralizing threat of punishment for having such impulses. Although, historically, these impulses have been accepted as sexual in nature, it is hereby proposed that the identification of such impulses as sexual, is seemingly, inaccurate. A new principle is here suggested, as follows:

In the psychoanalytic theoretical network, the attribution of the sexual instinct as crucial to symptom formation now needs to be replaced by the anger response as the true instrumentality, the actual core factor, in the transformation of the wish into the symptom.

It is proposed therefore, that the instinctual impulse implicated in the whole psychoanalytic symptom process is anger not sex or the sexual impulse, or even infantile sexuality, whereby according to Freud, symptoms occur because when repression fails in adult life, then infantile sexual impulses erupt out of such repression. Yes, it is true that a symptom can be cured by following sexual inhibition directly to disempowerment. But a sexual thwarted wish is no different from any other thwarted wish and leads to feelings of disempowerment, which will always generate anger. It is not the analysis of the repressed sexuality that will cure the symptom. Rather, it is only the analysis of repressed anger toward the *who*, toward the targeted object, the intended other person, that can ever realize the cure.

Again, it is proposed here that it is *only* the anger that accompanies the wish into repression, into the unconscious. And so long as the anger remains unconscious, and especially remains unconscious with respect to the memory of the original object–the *who* toward whom the anger was originally directed–the wish in the form of the symptom will sustain itself in this perverse or neurotic form, as a symptom.

In a related observation, Rangell (1959), posits that symptoms can reflect *either* libidinal *or* aggressive impulses. In addition, symptoms indicate changes in physical function symbolically seen in expressive body language and repressed instinctual impulses. It is interesting to note that in this definition, Rangell identifies *either* libidinal *or* aggressive drives as possible responsible variables in symptom formation; the operative terms being *either*, and *or*. This is important to note because the aggressive or anger impulse is frequently forgotten, underplayed, or even ignored by psychoanalytic theoreticians in favor of libido. Interestingly, release of anger is also pleasurable in the sense of the release from frustration. It is an expostulation, and as such shares with libido as well as with the wish, some commonality with respect to reflecting imperatives of the pleasure principle.

The blatant fact is that, concerning symptom cure, anger seems to be the missing emotion in the psychoanalytic theoretical landscape. Further, the emotion of *anger* is one of the few universal terms, along with the *wish, repression,* and the *memory of the symptom-context,* which I propose are the staples of the symptom cure-equation. I believe the truth of this formulation will become more apparent in the scientific analysis and clinical explication of the structure of the symptom and its cure, as the analysis in this book proceeds.

On the Nature of Basic Emotions

The basic nature of emotion (Plutchik, 1980, 1994), is another way of thinking about the propensity for the reflexive nature of emotions. In addition, the work by Kellerman (1979, 1980, 1983, 1990), implies that basic emotions also can be characterized by referring to the *personality of the emotion*. This consideration of the nature of basic emotions is important to include here because our focus on the emotion of anger invites more investigation into understanding the infrastructure of emotion generally.

The relevant factor of any basic emotion with respect to its "personality," concerns its basic tropism–that is to say, what it wants, or what it wants to do. For example, the basic nature of the emotion, fear, propels the person to flee. Fear, at its most basic reductionistic self, knows no other guiding principle, no other command, impulse, inclination, or dispositional tendency but to flee. Of course there are secondary, more complex social factors, which when brought to bear on the presence of fear, are able to modify, or alter the fleeing. Nevertheless, without these qualifiers, the basic nature of fear itself is simply to cause the person experiencing it to flee.

Basic emotions, therefore, it might be said, although developed in a social context, can be seen to be not of this social world. To underscore the point, to exaggerate it, it may be imagined that basic emotions exist in their basic raw state, outside civilization and outside socialization. They obey only what feels good to the person and are only based upon the imperative of the pleasure principle. Fear, feels good when the action of successful fleeing is implemented, and feels bad, when the possibility of fleeing is blocked.

The same is true of all other basic emotions. Anger is another example. Again, anger knows no civilization. Anger, seen either as a basic emotion or as a representative of a basic drive, causes the person to want to attack! It feels good if one can attack, and feels not so good if the basic need to express anger by attacking, is blocked. When anger can be expressed with respect to satisfying its basic impulse of attack, then again it can be said that the imperative of the pleasure principle has been realized. Parenthetically, I have stated elsewhere (Kellerman,1979), that because of social and psychological injunctions against confrontational aggression, anger is more likely repressed than any other emotion.

It is necessary to set forth this notion of the personality disposition of any basic emotion in order to further appreciate the process involved in the unlocking and curing of symptoms. This is true especially since the emotion of anger, it is proposed, plays an indispensable role in the formation of the symptom, and is one of the essential elements in the basic code of symptom formation.

How is Anger Managed?

When repression is not invoked and anger is directly expressed, there can be no symptom. It is only when anger is managed through repression that a transforming medium is created out of which a symptom forms. Most frequently, however, when a person experiencing a thwarted wish feels disempowered, and then as a result becomes angry, and cannot for whatever reason express the anger or even know it is there, it is then that such anger is captured by repressive forces of the personality. This entire process can occur in a fraction of a moment, so that the presence of the anger may never reach consciousness and therefore remains entirely outside of the person's awareness.

This reflexive process includes the anger, joined by the thwarted wish, and through repression becomes a translated product in the unconscious. This process of translation is embraced at the beginning with a thwarted wish, and at the end with a symptom. It is wish to symptom; that is, the anger remains unconscious and the wish is translated and surfaces as a symptom. What this means is that the anger remains in the repressive unconscious repository of the psyche and sustains the translated wish as symptom. It is as if the anger keeps the furnace stoked, so that the wish as symptom is continually lit.

The above comprises a brief sketch of the first phase of the symptom process with respect mostly to the underpinnings, the assumptions upon which are based the various axioms and constant terms of the symptom equation–the symptom-code.

In the next chapter, the structural formation of the symptom will be presented. The symptom formation referred to concerns only emotional-psychological symptoms that are not governed in the causative stage by organic brain lesions or any biochemical intervening variables. Further, and as stated earlier, symptoms that are engraved in the personality to the extent that they *become* the personality and not only an aspect of the personality, are not subject to the assumptions and axioms presented here. Most of the neurotic symptoms of everyday life that characteristically remain only facets of the personality, are solely the subject of this theoretical organization of the symptom-code, and of the practical application of this code in the cure of symptoms.

Chapter 3
The Symptom-Code and its Application

In the understanding of this system of assumptions, propositions and axioms regarding the formation, composition, and dissolution of emotional-psychological symptoms, there are essentially four phases that encompass the subject matter of symptom structure comprising the morphology and anatomy of symptoms. The first phase to be presented is actually a distillation of the exposition of the previous chapter

Phase 1: Before the Symptom Forms

1. The pleasure principle of life starts it–we want what we want.
2. The chief example of how the pleasure principle works in everyday life concerns the drive that people have to realize their wishes. The drives are considered the Freudian classical drives of libido and aggression, and the wish becomes the chief representative of the pleasure principle. It is the pleasure principle that contains the drives. When the pleasure principle is gratified we feel empowered.
3. When a wish is thwarted, however, frustration is experienced.
4. The result of a thwarted wish and its subsequent frustration, is a feeling of helplessness or disempowerment.
5. The natural response to disempowerment is the emotional reaction of anger which in itself is a pleasurable alleviation of the frustration and disempowerment. This anger reflex is natural because when someone is disempowered, anger frequently becomes the only way to feel reempowered.
6. The need to repress the anger is based on social and psychological injunctions against aggression.

Phase 2: Formation of the Symptom

When anger is repressed, as in the event of a thwarted wish, and the inability, incapacity, or inaccessibility of expressing the anger directly exists, one must then, in order to further appreciate this process, remember anger's basic personality.

That is, all anger wants to do, is attack. That is its basic nature. Therefore, when the anger is repressed, it can do nothing else but attack the self, the subject. It can do nothing else. The anger when repressed therefore, takes the self, attaches to the self, attacks the self.

This process of the target object morphing into the target-subject invokes another principle of emotion. Now to the proposition that each basic emotion has a unidimensional personality (anger, attacks; fear, flees), this must be added: *In order to be fully realized as an emotion, to be fully crystallized as an emotion, the emotion must be targeted toward or attach itself to a person-the object.* When the emotion cannot be directed to, or cannot "take" the object, then the emotion will just hang there, in a virtual state as it were, a condition that cannot be sustained because the emotion will not be fully realized without it attaching itself to a person-the subject becomes the object of the emotion. And here is the important moment. *When the self, the subject, is attacked by the repressed anger, then this moment constitutes the instant of conception leading to the birth of the subsequent symptom.*

Thus, the first step in understanding the genesis of symptom formation – and the organization of the symptom equation formulated in this volume – concerns the awareness that, on the face of it, *the thwarted wish* essentially deprives the pleasure principle of its reward. The second step emerges from *the sense of disempowerment regarding this thwarted wish.* The third step focuses on *the reflex of anger as a response to the state of disempowerment* in order to gain reempowerment. The fourth step is concerned with repression. When the anger, for whatever reason, cannot be directed toward its intended object, a person, a *"who," repression is therefore invoked and acts on the anger before the anger reaches consciousness.* Now the anger is repressed and unconscious. The fifth step occurs when the anger is repressed, because *accompanying the repression of the anger is the original wish* that was thwarted or denied. In this respect it should be remembered that one of Freud's seminal observations concerned his discovery that no wish will be denied. Therefore, the wish must, through repression, accompany the anger into the unconscious. There is no other way for the wish to be translated into the symptom if it is not, along with the anger, subject to repression. When the criterion of repression regarding both the anger and the wish, as material of the unconscious, is satisfied, only then is Freud's axiom that no wish will be denied revealed as a truth. Only then, is step 6 achieved; that is, that the wish is realized albeit neurotically or perversely as the symptom, or simply that the symptom appears as a symbol of the wish.

The originally denied wish therefore accompanies the anger, pressed as it were, into the unconscious–repressed together. Another of Freud's brilliant observations resonates here. Freud indicated that we love our symptoms, and this observation now makes sense. We love our symptoms, obviously, because symptoms are the wishes, fully gratified, though in symbolic form.

Review of the Six Steps of Symptom Formation in Phases 1 and 2

1. A wish is thwarted.
2. The subject is disempowered.
3. The subject becomes reflexively angry as a way of becoming reempowered.

4. If the anger cannot be directed toward its intended target–a person–then repression of the anger is invoked.

5. The original wish that was thwarted now accompanies the anger into the unconscious.

6. So long as the anger remains unconscious it stokes the repressive furnace, out of which emerges the symptom, which is the wish neurotically gratified in this transformed symbolic state.

A final seventh step involving the lifting of the symptom, to be discussed below is:

7. When the anger is made conscious, when the identified *who*–the person toward whom the anger was originally intended, is revealed–then it is predicted that the symptom will lift.

In the following section, these steps are formulated as a sequence of axioms.

Regarding Anger and Symptoms:

*Where there is repressed anger not only will there be a symptom, but there **must** be a symptom.*

Corollary: *Where there is no repressed anger, not only will there not be a symptom, but there **cannot** be a symptom.*

*Where there is a symptom, not only will there be repressed anger, but there **must** be repressed anger.*

Corollary: *Where there is no symptom, not only will there not be repressed anger, but there there **cannot** be repressed anger.*

Regarding the Wish:

A thwarted wish results in disempowerment feelings.

Disempowerment generates anger.

Anger that cannot be expressed directly, is repressed, thereby creating the moment of conception of the symptom.

In the process of repression, the wish–or rather the symbolization of the wish–joins with the anger in becoming unconscious.

The anger remains unconscious and acts to fuel the transformation of the wish into the symptom. Hence, no wish will be denied.

Phase 3: The All Important *Who*

Another axiom related to, but not solely relevant to symptom formation, concerns the issue of emotions and objects. The axiom is:

> *All emotion must take an object, and the object is always a person.*

The object is never a chair or a lamp. In trying to understand the symptom, one must always look for the person toward whom the anger was originally intended– the *who*.

Thus, the reaction of anger is always about a *who*. No emotion can just hang there suspended in mid air, as it were. Of course there are times when the other person, the object, is absent, or for whatever reason cannot be targeted with a direct expression of anger. Then, the self, the subject, becomes the substitute target of the anger–an internal target–so that as stated earlier, the object becomes the self. Thus, the emotion still has a person to attach to–the self. This then, is the process identified as the anger attacking the self and can be stated as an axiom, as follows:

> *When anger cannot be directed at the object toward*
> *whom it is intended, then the subject, the self, becomes*
> *the target, and thus the anger is repressed, and attacks*
> *the self.*

Phase 4: The Lifting of the Symptom

When the object of the anger, the *who*, is identified, and the anger toward the *who* becomes conscious, then the strength of the symptom is challenged and the symptom may even instantly lift. Thus, Freud's principle that *consciousness is curative*, is validated but *only* if it is the emotion of anger toward the *who* that becomes conscious. Nothing else can cure. Of course, in the course of psychoanalytic treatment, the unconscious must become conscious as the work proceeds. But it is proposed here that this process cannot cure anything unless it is anger toward the object, the *who*, that becomes conscious.

The axiom is:

> *Consciousness is curative only when what is made*
> *conscious refers to identifying anger toward an*
> *originally pre-repressed specific object–a specific*
> *'who'–a person.*

What emerges here is the ascendancy of anger and not sexuality or libido, as the salient variable in all symptom formation. Again, it is proposed that when libido is, in fact, implicated in symptom formation, it is not because of any impasse in the expression of the libido as it relates to sexuality, or because of a failure of repression, thereby permitting infantile sexual impulses to escape. Rather, it is here suggested that the implication of sexuality in symptom formation only exists because due to sexual impasses, failures, or frustrations, the subject becomes disempowered and fundamentally angry about it. Then because of the potential repression of the anger, a symptom will potentially appear. Clearly, in this formulation it is the anger and not the sexual impulse that is at the core of symptom formation.

Any symptom will be challenged more decisively, if after the *who* is identified and the anger toward this object, this *who*, becomes unrepressed, and if then the subject becomes actively involved in facing some aspect of the original problem–that is, the circumstance that involved the subject with the object in the first place (the symptom context)–then that kind of "doing" implementation will, in all likelihood, raise the probability of more decisively erasing the symptom. The axiom is:

> *When the anger toward the **who** is made conscious,*
> *then the symptom will become challenged or even lift.*
> *To further reinforce and fortify the cure of the symp-*
> *tom, some **doing** activity, some implementation, needs*
> *to take place involving the original symptom-context*
> *condition that first led to the need for the symptom.*

A final coda relates to chronic, resistive, deeply etched, or engraved symptoms–those that are not merely an aspect of the personality, but swallow the person whole, and become the personality. These are the symptoms that resist any psychotherapeutic modality. Other than symptoms based solely on biological causes, these are symptoms that have resulted from psychogenic major implosions of anger–so much so, that a symptom condition is wrenched into a permanent personality position. In such cases, it is suggested that the implosion of anger is really an implosion of the highest intensity of disempowerment and anger. This is basically rage or fury that creates an anger-debris that permeates the entire psyche. Such *inaccessible* symptoms usually can only be defeated when psychotropic medication is used along with psychotherapy.

In the following chapter, collateral issues of the symptom-code that fill out its context, will be presented. These issues include: the possibility that certain symptoms relieve tension while others increase it, and, an exposition of the psychology of withdrawal, as the arena in which symptoms are nourished, and flourish. Thus, these first four chapters of Part I of this volume, essentially comprise the contextual theoretical underpinning of the entire symptom-code utilized to penetrate and cure the symptom.

Definition of a Symptom: Infrastructure

A psychological/emotional symptom is the transformation of a thwarted wish (experienced as disempowering), into an involuntary symbolic configuration (a symptom). The symptom is formed by a reflexive anger response (as an attempt at reempowerment) toward the *who* – the person who thwarted the wish in the first place. Instead of being consciously expressed to this *who,* the anger, along with its connection to this *who*, then becomes repressed.

Implication

In this way, the transformed wish into the symptom satisfies Freud's discovery that in the psyche no wish will be denied – so that since the symptom is the wish (albeit in perverse or neurotic form), then indeed, we all love our symptoms (including those that are unpleasant or even painful), because they are informed in the unconscious as gratified wishes.

Chapter 4
On Wishes, Symptoms, and Withdrawal

Positive Versus Negative Symptoms

Are there some symptoms that become reinforced, sustained, and even intensified throughout the duration of the symptom episode, while others simply relieve tension? For example, the suffering of psychogenic migraines seems to be sustained, even fortified, throughout the duration of the episode. Such a symptom could be considered a negative one. On the other hand, an average compulsion, or perhaps even a severe one, when acted out, actually relieves tension; that is, the symptom episode (acting out the compulsion) produces a positive result for the person, a relief of tension.

Hence, we may consider that in view of this difference between the experience of sustained or intensified pain with respect to one kind of symptom, and the relief from pain with respect to another, that symptoms generally could be divided into two categories that we may operationally define as positive or negative. This labeling is based entirely on the person's experience of the symptom as painful or relieving, and not on any objective criteria of good or bad symptoms.

Where in the sequence of events that generated the symptom in the first place can we find what it is that makes for the difference between symptoms that ameliorate tension, versus those that exacerbate it?

The Wish and its Relation to Ameliorating and Exacerbating Symptoms

The answer to the question about what it is that determines whether a symptom is positive or ameliorating, or negative or exacerbating, concerns the person's original wish that was ultimately thwarted. If this original thwarted wish was a direct one–for a positive outcome of the wished-for scenario – then the ensuing symptom would be positive or ameliorating. The symptom would generate relief of tension. If, on the other hand, the thwarted wish was a negative one–that is, an indirect one, a wish to avoid something–then the ensuing symptom will be negative, or an exacerbating one where tension is increased. In either case, direct positive wish and relieving symptom, or indirect wish and painful symptom, the subject falls in love with the symptom, because, as discussed previously, the symptom is the wish satisfied, albeit in perverse or neurotic form, regardless of whether the symptom is relieving or painful.

Thus, the symptom is locked in, in perverse or neurotic form, and with respect to cure, it matters not whether the symptom is an ameliorative tension reducer, or a painful and tension exacerbating one. The cohesion of the symptom, its constraint or tight parameter, is impervious to reason of any kind. Rational or cognitive logical appeals or any kind of beseeching of the subject, or any kind of inducements–no matter how attractive–cannot have any curative effect on the symptom. None of these persuasions, seductions, or paradigmatic assumptions of normalcy, will ever have the slightest effect on the symptom. Not the slightest! These are reality oriented appeals and speak an entirely different language from that used by the symptom. The symptom does not respond to usual, manifest logic. The reason for such monumental failure on the part of reality-based appeals, approaches, or even admonitions toward the subject–regarding a relinquishment of the symptom— concerns the very nature of the symptom as an entity in a defined realm of the psyche. The symptom exists in the unconscious. It is condensed, a symbol for a wish; and more so, for a fully gratified wish (that we love), albeit in a translated, transformed, neurotic, or perverse configuration. It is proposed that the symptom can only be communicated with through the code presented here, involving an approach that aims to uncover the original wish by identifying the *who* toward whom the subject's repressed anger was originally directed.

Thus, the main theme, and the salient point to the present work, is to indicate that only when the subject becomes conscious of being angry toward this target person, will the symptom begin to dissolve. This is the only language understood by the symptom; that is, by the subject's unconscious. It is the language of wishes, repression, and the dynamics of the emotional mortar determining immutable laws of the connection between the subject and the *who*–the object, the other person.

It is in this sense that all of these reality-based genuine appeals, sincere approaches, and even severe admonishments, on the part of others toward the patient to relinquish the symptom, are all doomed to failure. The patient is almost always helpless to do anything voluntarily to assuage the symptom, because by definition, the symptom is beyond the patient's control. The symptom is a product or a ward of the unconscious, of repression. The symptom only exists because its host, the subject, when reacting with the symptom, is basically in a state of withdrawal.

The Symptom and the State of Withdrawal

In a non-clinical, non-pathological sense, withdrawal is actually, for all people, a natural phenomenon of everyday life, essentially a pause. It is a moment of inner rest. It is a solitary state. It is never authentically interactional, though it may be transferential.

Withdrawal is transferential insofar as the person in withdrawal can think, remember, or recall, any subject matter whatsoever that can be brought to mind. In withdrawal, rumination characterizes the state. Even when there are others around, when the subject withdraws, only perfunctory attention to others indicates moment to moment responses. There may be social niceties to honor, so that nodding to the other person as though one is actually attentive, is what is seen, but the subject is "not there"–was only ostensibly attentive. The subject is actually in withdrawal, pretending to be listening, but really only tuned to the self, only listening to the inner dialogue with someone the subject is thinking about. Or the subject may be listening to the ongoing monologue/dialogue–self to self.

The Line

A useful metaphor that illustrates this notion of withdrawal, is to imagine a line. *The Line* divides reality from fantasy; in front of *The Line* is reality, a "doing," an active place. There is no rumination in front of *The Line*. Rather, it is a place where one can be appealed to, approached, or even admonished, and usually with immediate effect, or at least with immediate response. There, in front of *The Line* is where logic reigns, and where genuine appeals, sincere requests, or even strong criticisms can be responded to. All of this is possible to achieve in front of *The Line*. All of these reality-based appeals, are in front of *The Line* data.

Behind *The Line* is defined as the arena of withdrawal. The fact that all people slip behind *The Line* several times each day, simply signifies that such brief withdrawal moments are rather successful attempts for all people to take a breather, to relax for a moment, to quickly recalibrate their balance, and then just as quickly to step out in front of *The Line* and resume their existence in the reality *doing* place.

In contrast, being behind *The Line*, is existing in a *non-doing* inactive place, of rumination and fantasy. It is a place to discharge one's feelings of anger, rage, fury, vengeance, depression, and miseries, and also one's conscious wishes, compensatory needs, and self-esteem tensions. Thus, in this fantasy place, behind *The Line*, frustrations can be played out, thereby relieving pressure.

A behind *The Line* withdrawal – especially in small doses – can also be seen as a condition of refuge, a sanctuary from worldly demands, expectations, and failures. This experience and place, behind *The Line*, in withdrawal, is where symptoms and the constituents of symptoms–the wish, repressed anger, and the *who* become fortified from above, from the level of consciousness–albeit in an arena of conscious or quasi-conscious withdrawal.

To the psychoanalysis of symptom composition–meaning the amalgam of the wish, repressed anger, and the *who*–is now added the collateral factors of the difference between ameliorating and exacerbating symptoms and their causative underpinnings. Along with this map of the psychoanalysis of symptoms is also added the notion of *The Line* (separating the arena of withdrawal – a non-doing place – from the region of reality – a doing place – and on the one hand, assessing normal withdrawal as the everyday experience of behind *The Line* pauses, compared to pathological withdrawal on the other hand, the ground for the incubation and sustaining of symptoms.

With these introductions, reintroductions, reviews, and summaries of symptom formation, and the blueprint to decode, unlock, and cure the symptom, a variety of clinical cases will be presented in Part II of this book. This blueprint, utilizing the set of axioms presented here, will be applied to these clinical cases and the systematic curing of symptoms will be demonstrated. All of the factors in the formation and ultimate penetration of the symptom will be focused upon with an aim of lifting or curing the symptom. These factors will include reference to:

1. The code for symptoms involving wishes, repressed anger, and the *who*;
2. Ameliorating and exacerbating symptoms;
3. The issue of the "doing" activity with respect to the original wish;
4. The issue of establishing *The Line* of withdrawal versus reality-doing.

Subsequently, with a lifting of the symptom, the most immediate and derivative result will show the subject moving from a behind *The Line* non-doing position, to a *doing* position, one that is in front of *The Line*.

It should be noted that symptoms do not just appear out of the blue. Each symptom is embedded in an understandable process; that is, a symptom context. The belief in the unknowability of symptom formation and the thrall of mystery or mystification with respect to the phenomenon of the appearance of symptoms, is simply a result of an absence of discovery, insight, and knowledge.

In the following section, Part II of this volume, the clinical application of the symptom-code will be utilized to demonstrate that the symptom, its formation, and process, is quite understandable, and not at all mysterious.

Part II
The Clinical Casebook:
Accessible Symptoms

Accessible symptoms are those that:

1. are not deeply engraved psychotic ones that have usurped the personality;
2. are not chronic;
3. are not chronically entrenched somatized ones;
4. are not derivative of an organic brain syndrome or genetic anomaly;
5. are not an example of a catastrophic rage implosion as a result of a condition of profound helplessness.
6. remain as an alien part to the psyche and so have not usurped the personality.

Chapter 5
Bottles Under the Bed:
A Case of Compulsion

A young boy, an only child of 11, reported "funny feelings" in his stomach, which he learned to "cure" (as he said), "by putting bottles under the bed." The case began with a phone call from his father, a psychiatrist, who stated that recently and quite accidentally, he noticed his son was placing "bottles under the bed."

The father said that he had consulted two other colleagues–a psychiatrist and a psychologist-the first of whom said medication was the treatment of choice because the symptom seemed too dense, while the psychologist suggested psychotherapy twice a week. The father had consulted with these colleagues only after he discussed the "bottles" symptom with his son. He also admitted to being embarrassed at not knowing how to approach this problem, especially since he was an experienced professional.

Apparently, his son told him that he began feeling funny in his stomach and quite naturally knew to put bottles under the bed. The boy reported that immediately upon placing the bottles under the bed, the funny feelings disappeared, as he kind of knew they would, and that then he instantly felt better, relieved.

The father, upon further questioning, ascertained that these feelings began several months earlier, and gradually increased in frequency. It was clear that the boy's funny feelings in his stomach and his method of curing these feelings, definitely qualified as a bona fide clinical psychological symptom. The father further indicated that neither he nor either of the consultants was able to determine or identify a cause for this symptom, and all were actually baffled about what seemed like something quite "strange and even weird."

The Initial Consultation

He was prompt. He was quite verbal and highly intelligent – an above average 11 year old. Play therapy did not at all seem appropriate here since he was eager to talk about the funny feelings as well as the bottles. Without even a single question posed to him, he volunteered that he knew his father had told me about his symptom and that he wanted to assure me that he was looking forward to getting rid of it – especially the funny feelings in his stomach – as well as looking forward to figuring out what it was all about, what it meant. He made it clear that he knew it meant *something*.

He started by saying, "I know it's completely connected." He explained that whenever he got a funny feeling in his stomach he would also immediately get a corresponding urge to put bottles under the bed. He confirmed what his father had initially reported–that as soon as the bottles were under the bed, he would get relief from the funny feelings. In response to my inquiry he also said that the feelings were not painful; that is, the funny feelings in his stomach were not painful feelings, they were just uncomfortable, "Like worried feelings," he volunteered, "butterflies".

Thus, in the first few minutes of the session, I confirmed that he was indeed suffering from a compulsive symptom eruption in the ostensible absence of any obsessive preceder. What seemed to be happening to him was that he had some generalized somatized condition that he was able to cure through a compulsive, highly symbolic act, so that in its realized ritual, he got relief by temporarily dissolving the symptom–"It was like magic," he said.

In this sense of the patient's description of the symptom, the symptom itself could be considered to be an aspect of a process rather than an isolated event. First, the funny feelings were preceded by some still undetermined stimulus, and second, there was the compulsion to dissolve the funny feelings by putting bottles under the bed. In addition, according to this boy, the cure worked every time. One of the poignant moments occurred when he spontaneously said, "It's starting to happen more and more now, and I'm worried about it more."

Applying the Symptom-Code

The three major constituents of the symptom code presented in Part I of this volume, include: 1. a thwarted wish; 2. repressed anger regarding the subject's inability or powerlessness to reverse the thwarted wish; 3. Identifying the *who*, the person toward whom the anger was originally intended.

The prediction is that if we are able to unravel all three, by definition, repression will lift and the symbol of the symptom will reveal itself, and the symptom will then become reconstituted into the original wish, made conscious.

Therefore, in the face of this conundrum of a boy placing bottles under the bed to relieve funny feelings in his stomach, and based upon the symptom-code, the question is: What do we already know even before we begin our direct therapeutic process or direct inquiry with him? We know:

1. He had a wish he couldn't realize; that is, each symptom begins with a thwarted wish. Our question is, what was that wish?
2. He was angry. Who was the someone with whom he was angry? This question is based on two principles – the first is: Where there is a symptom there must be repressed anger; and, second, all emotion, including anger, takes an object, a person;
3. Hence he is angry at one particular person, and again, who is that *who*?

When faced with any symptom, therefore, applying this understanding, will transform the most complicated, seemingly baffling symptom into a form that can be immediately understood, and of course, managed. The symptom-code presented here permits an approach to this or any such symptom so that an efficient penetration of the very infrastructure of the symptom can be made–to its very core.

In this case, an entry point in the treatment and decoding of his symptom could begin almost anywhere within the terms of the symptom-code: seeking the *who*; seeking the pivotal original event (the symptom context) containing the *who*; or, trying to make conscious the anger itself. In addition, each element of the symptom story, of course, is subject to scrutiny. What kind of bottles are they? What do they contain? Whose bed do the bottles go under? Basically, no assumptions can be made about such questions until detailed information is provided by the patient.

Ultimately, it is important for the patient to know that he did have a wish, and to know what that wish was. Furthermore, it is important for the symbol, that is, the symptom, to be understood. The subject needs to see that "bottles under the bed" means something, and to know what that something is. That is, that *"bottles under the bed" relates to a specific feeling (anger), about a specific person (the 'who'), regarding something that was blocked or thwarted (a wish).*

I decided to begin by asking him when the symptom began, when he first noticed it. He said that it was several months earlier when he started feeling the funny feeling in his stomach and that then he began putting bottles under the bed. As soon as he put the bottles under the bed, then like magic, the funny feeling disappeared. He added that at first the funny feeling came only occasionally, but that now it was more frequent–"all the time, in fact"–and he was, for the first time, worried that he would not be able to control it and that it would "just keep getting worse and worse."

He claimed, "it just happened"; that is, he was saying the symptom just appeared and that by implication there was no pivotal event that started it, at least that he was aware of. In contrast, I was tenacious in pursuing an actual pivotal event, which he assumed he never had, but which I assumed we simply had not yet identified. After working for a while on trying to pin down some event occurring prior to the onset of the symptom, he casually mentioned that some time ago (he thought it was before he had his first funny stomach feeling) he remembered that his parents had a "humongous fight, a tremendous argument." He had never before heard them fight like that. He said: "They were both red in the face and they were shouting to each other about divorce." What seemed to scare him was that his father's threat to divorce his mother bothered him, while his mother's threat was, "only a counter to it," and he further said: "I think it was made in self-defense."

I immediately considered this boy's recollection of his parents' fight to qualify as a possible pivotal stimulus that may have originally triggered his symptom and constituted the symptom context. At that point, I shifted to a focus on the *who*. It is clear that an 11 year old boy's repertoire of objects (important people in his life), is probably rather limited: parents, siblings, a friend or two, a teacher, another relative. In this case, he had no siblings, and further, in describing his friendships, relationships, relatives, and teachers, it seemed unlikely that any of them would qualify as the *who*. His mother and father remained as the possible culprits. Yet, only one, either mother or father, would ultimately be the one *who*. Emotion takes an object–singular!

Thus, fundamentally, he would have been angry at one of them. Based on the sobering effect his father's declaration of divorce had on him, my theory was that the *who* was his father. To further validate this hypothesis and not assuming I knew which bed he put the bottles under, I then asked him which bed it was. He answered as though his answer would have been obvious, as though to say, "of course." He said, "My parents' bed."

And now the puzzle was beginning to coalesce, even in the absence of the previously recommended twice per week sessions or the use of medication. So far, we only needed knowledge of the symptom-code. And now it was increasingly evident that the symptom itself would be under pressure; that is, he and I were beginning a partnership that would likely also begin to undermine the symptom by diluting his very own resistance to knowing something important that he was concealing–repressing, especially from himself. This self-same resistance, like all resistance, designed to support repression, would begin to lift in the face of making the unconscious, conscious; that is, in making conscious the anger toward the *who*. In this case, his resistance was, of course, supporting repression of the anger toward the *who* – that person who, in his unconscious, he held responsible for the thwarting of his original wish.

Then I finally addressed the issue of what might be considered oedipal geographic archaeology. "Where under your parent's bed do you place the bottles?" I asked. "Is it always in one place, or are the bottles placed anywhere at all?" Since an emotion, like anger, takes a single object, I was sure he didn't place the bottles in the middle, under the bed. It would have to be either on his mother's or his father's side of the bed.

"Under my father's side," he immediately answered. "Always," I asked? "Yes, always. Only on my father's side."

With this answer it became clear that his father was definitely the *who*. Now, I wanted to know more about the bottles. I had not assumed I knew anything about them. I asked him about them, asked whether size mattered as in whether they were big or small, or the type of bottle. To this, he said, "They all have to be medicine bottles or about medicine. Some are big and some are smaller."

That answer was the last piece of the puzzle revealing the entire picture. The symptom and the whole process of the symptom formation of "bottles under the bed," became clear. We would now be able to reconstitute the original wish and make it clear and conscious to him.

Understanding the Symptom

He was an only child and he needed his family to remain in tact. His focus was to get his father to love his mother, a positive, direct wish. Thus, the positive wish produced a symptom process that was relieving; that is, a compulsive symptom ultimately relieved tension. The symptom, beginning with some stimulus that produced a funny feeling in his stomach ended in the automatic, compulsive act of putting bottles under the bed and thereby immediately relieving the funny feeling.

When divorce was threatened, especially passionately threatened, he then felt his world was about to be shattered. He became frightened and it was this fear, this apprehension, that occupied his consciousness. However, the salient factor was not the fear; rather, what was crucial was his anger toward the *who*, his father. The main point here is that in contrast to his conscious fear, his anger was unconscious. He could not bring himself to know he was angry at his father. He loved his father. Apparently, the conflict between the love and the anger was too great. Therefore, he had not been aware of his unconscious anger and the devastating emotional and psychological effect it was having on him. It was his anger that needed attention. Trying to cure his symptom by focusing on his fear could never cure the symptom. It's never about the fear!

He believed his mother loved his father but that his father probably didn't love his mother. It became clear that he had formed this opinion because his mother was more demonstrative with her affection than was his father, whom he described as "more quiet." And therefore, the fact that he believed it was his father who was threatening the integrity of his world–actually threatening his wish of keeping the family in tact–kept feeding this boy's anger because he felt disempowered in the face of his anticipated crumbling world.

Furthermore, that the bottles under the bed were always medicine bottles made this symbol quite easy to understand. Medicine is used to cure. Thus, he placed these medicine bottles under his father's side of the bed, obviously because it was his father who needed to be cured of not loving his mother. Then, of course, when cured, his father *would* love his mother. Hence, no divorce, and his wish for the family to remain whole, would be realized. His world would then be undisturbed, his security protected. Then, and only then would the unconscious anger disappear because he would have no identifiable tangible reason to be angry. To the contrary, he would now, with his wish met, feel quite empowered. With empowerment, there is no anger, and therefore, no symptom.

Thus, whenever he placed these "medicine" bottles under the bed on his father's side all his funny stomach feelings disappeared. This, rather ingenious boy, who was curing his father over and over again, also satisfied the definition of a Freudian repetition-compulsion which relieves the immediate tension but never solves the problem. In this boy's case, the problem concerned the complex issue of the wish for an intact family interacting with his anger toward his father, as well as a repetitive compulsive attempt on his part to cure his father, and in so doing, also continuing, of course, to cure himself.

Thus, this repetitive compulsive ritual of putting bottles under the bed could never solve the actual problem. All it could do was symbolically cure his father, and then again, the logic of the medicine bottles was itself entirely symbolic. This was so, because the bottles didn't actually need to contain medicine. Actually, most of them were empty, or nearly empty. The whole ritual was symbolic. In its symbolic nuance, in the behind *The Line* fantasy, imaginary medicinal fumes, medicinal vapors really, would waft up from under the bed, through the mattress, and into his father's corpus–thereby curing his father. Thus, putting bottles under the bed gave him a good feeling, dissolved the funny feeling in his stomach, and produced a relief of tension.

Each step of the unraveling of this fully developed symptom was shared with the patient, all within the first session. He was an astute boy and eager to know what the symptom was all about. Our work reached the point where he understood that he was angry at his father, and why he was angry. He now knew that because of his father's outburst during his parents' fight, he himself was feeling weak (disempowered) and this was devastating him because it thwarted his wish to keep the family intact. That he was trying to cure his father with fantasy medicine, astounded him. He was now also amazed at the logic of his symptom, and the whole symptom process.

His understanding included: an awareness of his wish, and his frustration about it; his unconscious anger; and the identification of the *who*, his father–the object about whom he was angry. He actually said that knowing it all "was amazing," indicating also that it was far more interesting to him than even the original, seemingly unfathomable mystery of the symptom itself.

At the end of the session he acceded to my request that we have one session with his parents. When later we convened that session, his parents remembered their fight but assured him that the fight was unimportant and that they never intended to divorce or anything like that. In fact, they intended to be together always. His father verbalized his love both for his wife and for him, and both parents were entirely believable in their claims of loyalty, fidelity, and love.

This family session further satisfied one of the criteria for the permanent dissolution of a symptom; that is, that *doing* something in front of *The Line* that directly relates to the original thwarted wish will more decisively erase the symptom. Even several years later, this boy's symptom had entirely lost its power and had never reappeared.

The question of why this boy reacted so strongly to the event of his parents' fight, and any other more deeply etched conflicts, could be reserved for further therapeutic work.

Chapter 6
Holes: A Case of Body Delusion

An elderly man of 80 was committed to a city hospital facility for observation. He presented with "bizarre behavior," and a variety of symptoms including depression, and body delusion. He was quite erudite, and was a published poet. As his day-job, he had been gainfully employed in the needle trades while continuing to publish his poems in various periodicals. At the time of the recent onset of his symptoms he was still at the same job he had held for decades. All in all, the patient was a robust octogenarian whose full complement of symptoms included depression, impotence, body delusion, and complaints of a continuously queasy stomach.

His depression became evident when be could no longer get to work on time, and began complaining of his great problem – that of getting out of bed in the morning. He conveyed the idea that he also began feeling dispirited and demoralized. He said he had wanted to cry but couldn't. His impotence was of concern to him because he said he was neglecting his current common-law wife. His wife had died some years before. He claimed to have had an uninterrupted active sexual life all of his life until "this tragedy" befell him.

Furthermore, the notation in the hospital chart of "bizarre symptom" referred to his body delusion. Apparently, this man felt there were holes all over his body–holes you could see through. The queasy stomach was also unexplained, except for his pronouncement that "it was all the time," meaning it never abated. In disgust, he said, "It's no good any more–nothing is good."

The Initial Consultation

The patient was a nice looking man. He was obviously intelligent and appreciated the opportunity to have the interview. He said he felt depressed, but his acute interest in our meeting did not indicate that he was in any way chronically depressed. He seemed to be interested in many things, while his current feeling of hopelessness was just that: current and acute, and did not seem at all chronic or entrenched.

The first two issues he reported concerned his depression and his body delusion of holes. Contrary to how he was behaving, he explained that he was not interested in anything anymore, and that nothing mattered anyway because his body was full of holes. "These holes that you can even see through them," is how he put it. I asked him if the holes were all over his body or if they were located only in one spot. My interest in asking this question had less to do with any particular aim and more with creating an ongoing discussion. He said the holes were all over his body and that he knew it meant he was "through." By "through," he explained that it meant his life no longer mattered and that he was now a useless person.

He reported that his wife had "departed" (died) several years earlier and that for the past few years he had "taken up" with a very nice lady. He also un-self-consciously reported that he had been sexually active all of his life but that now he could no longer function "in the same way." He also confirmed that he was continuously employed in the same job for all of his working life. In total, he confirmed everything on his intake chart, and further, filled it in with greater detail. He also spoke at length about his first love, poetry, and indicated that he was a published writer.

With respect to his family, he had two sons—one a "very successful lawyer," and the other, a struggling actor who frequently needed to be subsidized. He claimed to be close to both sons and was in constant touch with them. He followed this discussion by wondering what had happened to him. He didn't know why he suddenly became depressed nor what had happened for him to become so plagued "with all this craziness."

When referring to the "terrible feeling" in his stomach, the patient pointed further down, toward his genitals, and did this, what might be considered *a displacement downwards,* whenever he again, referred to his stomach. He sighed deeply and said, "Look what happened to me."

Applying the Symptom-Code

As in the previous chapter, what was needed here was information regarding the three salient components of the symptom code – information about: (1) the thwarted *wish*; (2) repressed *anger* regarding the subject's inability or powerlessness to reverse the thwarted wish; (3) identifying the *who*, the person toward whom the anger was originally intended.

Again, the prediction was that if we would be able to identify all three, as well as help the patient become aware and conscious of them, then by definition, repression would lift and the symbol of the symptom would reveal itself (the symptom would then become reconstituted into the original wish made conscious).

Therefore, in the face of this conundrum of an elderly, impotent, depressed man, with a continuously queasy stomach, and a delusion about holes all over his body that could be seen through, and based upon the symptom-code, the question became: What did we already know even before we began our direct therapeutic process or direct inquiry with him? We knew:

1. He had a wish he couldn't realize; that is, each symptom begins with a thwarted wish: What was that wish?
2. He was angry: Who was the someone with whom he was angry? This question is based on two principles. First, where there is a symptom there

must be repressed anger, and second, all emotion including anger, takes an object, a person.

3. Hence, he was angry at one particular person, and again, who was that *who*? Who is the person with whom he was angry?

When faced with any symptom therefore, applying this code, this understanding, will reduce the most complicated, seemingly baffling symptom, into a proportion that can be immediately understood, and of course, managed. The symptom-code presented here, permits an approach to this or any such psychological symptom, so that an efficient penetration of the very infrastructure of the symptom can be made.

Ultimately, in this patient's case, a major clue to his symptomatology, perhaps because he was a poet, proved to be a play on words. In addition, it was clear that his symptoms did not materialize out of the clear blue sky. Someone got into his guts and caused him to have that queasy stomach and all the other symptoms that had him in its grip. He was dispirited and demoralized.

We carefully spent the remainder of the interview going over, step by step, his activities at the time immediately before he wakened one morning with his depression. Thus, my decision in this case was to at once seek a pivotal event. He then reviewed his work relationships and his relationship with his common-law wife. None of these seemed to yield any sort of event containing the person nor the crisis; that is, until he began discussing his sons.

The patient finally revealed that he was not feeling good about his lawyer son. Apparently, what had occurred during this pivotal event, left the patient in a terrible emotional state. He had called this son to ask for a loan because he needed to help the other son with rent payments. Such requests had also occurred in the past and were always responded to favorably by this lawyer son. This time, however, our patient was summarily dismissed and his son, without even ending the conversation with a familial "goodbye," simply put down the receiver–hung up.

We discussed this for a few minutes. It seemed to me that the patient perhaps had called at an inopportune time and his son, without realizing the effect of treating the call the way he did–that is, allegedly abruptly, and in the absence of any consideration or even respect–created in his father a terrible feeling of rejection, even humiliation. As it turned out, the patient's sense of humiliation became the sine que non of this interaction and of its effects.

It seemed obvious that the *who* had now been identified. Additionally, it seemed also obvious that he was angry at his attorney son and that it was precisely this anger that he avoided acknowledging–at all costs. He simply didn't want to know about it. He could feel humiliated and subsequently depressed about this humiliation, but would not allow himself to understand, to be conscious of, his deep anger toward this son. Apparently, he did not want to consciously institutionalize the breach with his son that was already fulminating, albeit unconsciously.

No, it was not his sexual repression that caused these symptoms. There may not even have been a sexual repression. What was, however, in all likelihood the problem, was that the swallowing of his anger, the repression of his anger, anaesthetized his sexuality, his libido, so that he could no longer feel sexually interested. It was the anger that was the emotional culprit, the repressed anger toward the *who*-the attorney son. The principle may be stated as: *Where there is anger, there is no libido.*

Now each element of the symptom-code had fallen into place. His *wish* was for his son to respect him and even show respect with indulgence, and in addition, to offer the loan without any ambivalence or hesitation whatsoever. This was the wish that was probably thwarted. Faced with this situation, he then probably felt helpless, and immediately disempowered.

It can be predicted that to the disempowerment, he felt *angry*. As stated earlier, the psychology of such a connection between a feeling of disempowerment and the emotion of anger is really quite logical. When one is disempowered, there are times when the only way to become reempowered is by becoming angry. This particular understanding of the connection of empowerment and anger also reveals that the emotion of anger is an empowering emotion–a conclusion that is usually not understood because of the tendency to see anger as negative reaction.

Thus, the wish this patient had for his son to cooperate, was dashed. He became angry, but repressed the anger because: (1) he was humiliated by the manner of the rejection; and, (2) because to know he was angry would have been a humiliation on top of a humiliation. His lawyer son was the *who*, that was for sure.

After discussing his feelings of this son's rejection of him, he then readily admitted to seeing the connection between what his son did and his own subsequent depressed feeling. Yet, although he saw this connection, nevertheless, he still was not in touch with his actual anger toward his son. He agreed that he was disappointed in his son, and he agreed also that he was feeling awkward about again calling his son. But he couldn't quite face his anger, or even rage, toward this son. It was only gradually that he began to notice that whenever he replayed the event of his rejection by his son, he got "that terrible feeling." I assured him that at the bottom of this terrible feeling he was not only dissatisfied and disappointed in this son, but that he was justifiably angry at him because, as I put it: "You felt he was rude, that he was disrespectful, and you were probably dissatisfied–don't you think?"

The idea that his son may have been rude and disrespectful, and as a result, the patient may have been dissatisfied in response to this rejection, very much helped him to get a bit more in touch with his anger at his son. The rationale here was that one can have anger at rudeness but not as easily feel angry at being rejected. Feeling rejected is worse with respect to one's ego, to one's self-respect, than feeling angry. Being angry at rudeness, is more socially acceptable and does not as easily implicate one's ego with regard to feeling humiliated. It's really a matter of easing into it.

"Okay," he said. "Yes, he was rude and he should never be rude because I raised him to be a good boy. So, yes, I am mad at him because maybe now he thinks because he's a big lawyer he doesn't have to be nice to the smaller people." After a pause, he said, "Well, no, maybe it's not that. Maybe it's just that he doesn't need me anymore–like a son needs a father. Like maybe he's the father, and I'm the son now. No good, no good."

Understanding the Symptom

The patient needed his younger struggling son not be struggling. Thus, his fundamental, primary wish did not concern the successful older son. In this sense, even though it seems that his wish was for the successful son to provide the necessary funds, nevertheless, this was not his primary wish. His primary wish was directed to the younger son who needed the subsidy. The patient needed to provide this son with the subsidy so that the tension of "where his next dollar was coming from, could be less." Thus, this father's wish was an indirect one; that is, he wished that his younger son could avoid poverty. The wish was directed toward a goal defined as avoiding something. Because of this kind of avoidant or indirect wish, the symptoms the father developed were troublesome, painful, and surely did not relieve tension. In contrast, had the wish been focused or cast in a positive direct way, then the symptom, whatever it would have turned out to be, would have relieved tension rather than sustained it.

In this patient's case, his repressed anger regarding the humiliation he felt, both because he was insulted by his son's dismissiveness and because he was now unable to help his needy younger son, seemed likely to be related to the symptom of his impotence. In addition, apparently he had swallowed so much anger that he also became depressed. The repressed anger, of course, true to its nature, attacked the self. The symptom of impotence also could be seen as a side effect of the depression because, as previously stated, his repression of anger, in all likelihood, anesthetized all libidinal inclinations and sensations. Since the psychological principle governing such impotence suggests a high negative correlation between anger and libido, then apparently, anger and libido do not coexist, especially within normal parameters.

The third symptom of an unrelenting queasy stomach seemed also related to this libido problem and to his impotence. The clue to this connection of a queasy stomach and impotence, was his pointing to his genital area whenever he mentioned the stomach symptom. In psychoanalytic terms, this kind of slip-of-the-gesture refers to a displacement of focus. In the case of this patient, his pointing to his genitals when he was referring to his stomach is considered a displacement from his genitals to his stomach, or the other way around–downwards or upwards, as the case may be–meaning, that something is not right down there (genitals), and is instead, feeling bad, up here (stomach).

Finally, perhaps the most interesting, even fascinating symptom of all, concerns his body delusion regarding "holes" one could see through that he believed existed throughout his body. It is the particular meaning of holes that requires a new synthesis, without which, it becomes virtually impossible to understand the delusion.

The main point concerns the ubiquitous wish we all have to be adequate, to be empowered, in essence, to be whole. And this is what was meant by the aforementioned "play on words." In this case, "hole," also meant "whole." When the patient felt inadequate, after being humiliated, the feeling of needing to be *whole* turned into a feeling that there were *holes* in his body. The delusion of holes in his body was simply his way of expressing his inadequacy, defeat, shame, unwhole-ness, embarrassment, and so forth. So long as this condition of inadequacy would be sustained, would in turn constitute the corresponding length of time that he would believe in his "holes." And this condition of inadequacy refers to the reten-tion of repressed anger regarding a *who*.

The point at which his anger toward the *who*, his attorney-son, became con-scious, was also the point at which his entire symptom-syndrome experienced its first death knell. That is to say, that in the first place, his entire symptom syn-drome was a behind *The Line* drama. So long as this drama with its repressed anger and the identity of the *who* remained repressed, he remained in withdrawal, behind *The Line*. When he became conscious of his anger toward his attorney-son, however, he then stepped out in front of *The Line*, out of withdrawal, and into a reality *doing* place. In this new condition, in front of *The Line*, his symptoms could not survive.

In this case, the example of the entire syndrome of depression, impotence, queasy stomach, and body delusion of holes, demonstrated the powerful effect of symbolism. This patient's entire syndrome was all symbolic, and had him in the grip of what was called "bizarre" symptomatology.

When the picture began to clear up for him, he was astounded at how he had sacrificed himself in order to avoid knowing how angry he was–and even that he was, in fact, angry in the first place. Even though he said he felt "a little renewed," nevertheless, I asked him to do something that related to the original problem. This was the final step in more decisively defeating the symptom. I requested a joint meeting with his attorney-son. After much resistance and a corresponding amount of my persistence, he agreed.

The point that most astonished him was the word play of "hole" and "whole." I appealed to him to trust the interpretation by reminding him that he was a poet and that such word plays probably would be more germane to him than they would be to an average layperson, that he would be more likely to unconsciously engage in such word plays than others who were not as connected as he was with words. He liked that explanation, and it won him over to the interpretation.

His son did attend the joint session and explained that he had not even realized that the conversation went the way that his father had experienced it. He further explained that he was in a meeting and couldn't talk, fully intending to return the call. As it happened, events kept the return call on a back burner. The patient was relieved at his son's apparently authentic and sincere explanation. The son, on the other hand, was horrified at not being informed, at his father's request, about his father's hospitalization.

The end result was that, through the father's good offices, the son gladly offered the subsidy to his brother. Soon thereafter, the patient was released from the hospital. His entire hospitalization lasted three weeks. He was symptom-free.

The family session was important because it satisfied one of the criteria for the permanent dissolution of the problem; that is, that *doing* something in front of *The Line* that directly relates to the original thwarted wish, will more decisively erase the symptom.

Chapter 7
Symptoms Based Upon
Feelings of Rejection:
Strangling, Sweats, and Death

In the following three cases, each patient experienced feelings of rejection, and developed symptoms directly related to such feelings. In the first case, the patient developed intrusive fantasies of strangling his girl friend. In the second case, the patient developed night sweats, so that his bedding and pajamas needed to be changed because they were soaking wet. In the third case, the patient developed mortality fears and could not prevent herself from obsessively focusing on the eventual prospect of her own death.

In all three cases, the severity and intensity of the symptom was a clue as to the respective causative stimulus of each. In each case, it was relatively easy to identify these ostensible causative stimuli. In this respect, the intrusive strangling thought, the physiologically intense response of sweating, and the terribly obsessive, incessant thought of death, were all related to identifiable pivotal events–the symptom context–containing other significant people in each patient's life.

A Case of Intrusive Thoughts of Strangling

A single man in his 50's, was always finding new women to date and so his social calendar was always busy. Yet at no time did he ever develop a long-standing relationship. The duration of any of his relationships was always a function of how much his date would focus on him. If he could talk about himself at length, he liked it better and he would be interested in seeing her again. If his date demonstrated impatience, or insufficient interest in him, then the first date with that person would be the last.

This man's early history was such that his primitive sense of the nature of relationships, was understandable. He was one of two siblings with a father who was exceedingly impatient. In order for him to talk to his father, he would need to think through what it was he wanted to say and then blurt it out quickly so as not to either bore or anger his father. In contrast, his mother was an indulgent woman who gave him the feeling that he was special.

Although he never really felt comfortable with his father, ironically he grew to be just like him–impatient, intolerant, impulsive, inattentive to others, insensitive, and uninvolved. His modus operandi was to seek a woman who would indulge him as his mother had done.

He was a successful businessman with a great deal of energy. His clients appreciated his no-nonsense style. When his impatience in interpersonal affairs was a detriment to his relationships, in business this impatience translated into an efficient style that gave his clients the feeling that they were in good hands. They got what they wanted, and in record time. The patient frequently boasted about all the compliments he got with regard to this, what he called his "problem-solving style." He said, "None of this emotional stuff, just solve the problem–get it?"

The Initial Consultation

At the first consultation, this man immediately reported that since the previous weekend he had been feeling anxious all the time. What had happened is that his date and he were in her apartment and he suddenly got the thought that he wanted to strangle her. He reported that he felt "funny" the entire evening. The feeling continued after dinner, as well as at the theater, reaching its zenith finally in an emotional and suddenly anxious crescendo that overcame him when they were ending the evening at her apartment. The anxiety he was feeling seemed to have been generated by what he said was his impulse to act out a thought of wanting to strangle her. It was then that he immediately felt anxious, and the anxiety only subsided when he excused himself and fled.

He indicated that the week preceding this date, he was on a date with a different woman, and began having a similar feeling, although at that time the anxiety was just a discomfort. He stated that the whole thing worried him, and he wondered whether he could ever again be with a woman without having such thoughts.

Applying the Symptom-Code

It appeared that in this case, identifying the three main terms of the symptom-code with respect to this man's dynamics, was a relatively simple task: Each of his dates was the *who*. It was they toward whom he was angry. He reported in the first session that in both cases each woman held forth extensively but not at all about him. "They talked and talked," is how he put it. Apparently, they made no room at all for him to refer to himself. From his narcissistic vantage point this man was in a severe state of feeling deprived of admiration, of feeling deprived of narcissistic supplies. In other words, he needed these women to talk about him either exclusively or almost exclusively. Instead they talked about themselves as well as about other things–everything and anything but him.

It became obvious that he was quite angry with his dates regarding the focus of these discussions. His *wish* was that these women would indeed talk to him about himself, which they didn't. Since they did everything but focus on him, he became impatient and intolerant, and in addition, apparently *repressed most or even all of his anger.* After his wish to be focused upon was thwarted, and after his anger became repressed, then the very next thing that occurred was the appearance of his intrusive thought of strangling.

Of course his anxiety about it all, and his stampede out of his date's apartment, and according to him, "out of the relationship altogether," was a clinical indication that his thought of strangling was really only an expression of his anger–an alien thought–and not in any way relevant to a bona fide acting out of strangling.

Understanding the Symptom

This patient was having a solipsistic-like episode; that is, he was simply narcissistically impatient. His solipsism was not just a function of his belief that only the self can be known-his self, that is,-but also a function of his desire, his wish, for others to demonstrate the same belief, namely, that the only information that could be important was information about him. Thus, these dates were boring him to death. Yet, the only way for him not to be bored would be to have all the focus throughout the conversation on him. As noted earlier, *bored*, is often one of the many code words for *anger*.

Assuming repression of his anger, then it would also follow that the anger was, as is its nature when repressed, directed at the self; thus, a symptom was to be expected. In this patient's case, the symptom that appeared, was an urge to strangle his date. Essentially the intrusive thought of strangling represented his wish, even his fervent wish, and more urgently, his narcissistically fervent wish, for her to stop talking about herself or whatever else she was talking about, and to begin talking about him. His problem was not at all that he was in danger of strangling her. His problem was that he couldn't get her to talk about him; in other words his wish for her to talk about him, was thwarted.

Based upon this understanding of his strangling thought, the prediction would be that as soon as the woman began talking solely about him, all thoughts of strangling would disappear. Thus, the strangling thought was another way for him to say, "Stop talking unless you only talk about me." On his next date with a new person, there was no sign of the strangling thought because his date was quite interested in him and really pretty much only talked about him. As a result he was not bored (angry), and therefore didn't need to repress any anger, and his wish was fully realized. Hence, no symptom.

On the face of it, it seems that his wish was direct (he wished for his dates to talk about him) yet, in actual practice, his wish was really an indirect one. It was actually a so-called negative wish: He wanted them (he wished them), to stop talking about other things. In contrast, a wish that would have been proactive and direct would be simply for them to talk about him and not focus on an indirect wish. In this sense, his symptom of the strangling thought made him anxious, and either sustained or sometimes even increased his tension. It was the dread of rejection that was the nub of it all. Then in a behind *The Line* drama, he developed his symptom.

Thus, a direct wish produces a symptom that relieves tension while an indirect one reflects an indirect route to the primary wish, and will produce a symptom that sustains or increases tension. The strangling fantasy reflected the indirect wish—one that represented an indirect route to the primary wish, thus exacerbating his tension and worrying him.

A Case of Nighttime Sweats

A man in his 30's suddenly began awakening, to find himself soaked in sweat and somewhat disoriented. His wife would help him change his pajamas and then she would change the bedding. He had always been a good sleeper and this symptom had never before appeared.

He consulted a physician after the third or fourth such sweating episode. All of his tests were negative, and he was told that these night sweats were probably a function of some emotional or psychological problem.

He and his wife had been married for a decade. They were a very social couple, and were also actively involved in their respective large extended families. They had not seriously contemplated having children and had always "put it on the back burner." He was an attorney and his wife was an instructor at a culinary institute. They were affluent, lived in an elaborate, opulent apartment, and would spend weekends at their country home.

Their sexual history had been problematic. He was shy, and she was "high strung." Thus, the conjugal part of the relationship seemed complicated and by implication, probably tense, or at least, compromised. In addition, in the recent past they had begun to bicker, and despite his love for her, the relationship seemed, in this respect, to be getting worse and not better. This, despite their avowed promise to one another from the beginning of their relationship, to try to be nice to, and to accommodate each other. They would occasionally repeat this vow, especially after some of their bickering episodes.

None of these promises had the strength to withstand the quality in his wife that he found most difficult, her stubbornness, and the quality in him that she found most difficult, his excessive compliance. Thus, although he expressed love for her, he also indicated that he experienced an abject inability to have any sway with her. He began to feel that his ineffectiveness was becoming more of his typical part of their relationship, while generally speaking, she was becoming more of the assertive or dominant one. He claimed she was "an angel otherwise," even though he reported that on occasion she also began making jokes about these night sweats. She would tell him that the night sweats were like bed-wetting or crying episodes, and then would laugh, and say that these were only jokes, and that a sense of humor is what was needed.

In contrast, he thought the sweating episodes presaged some terrible disease that was developing within, notwithstanding the doctor's clean bill of heath. He also considered the possibility that he may have had terrible dreams but not remembered them. He was, in his desperation to understand his symptom, grasping at straws. His wife disagreed and tried to persuade him that there was nothing wrong with him physically, and in addition, said she didn't think his sweats were a result of bad dreams.

The Initial Consultation

"I think it all started because I mentioned that maybe we should start thinking about having a family of our own–meaning having a baby." This was just about the last comment he made at the end of the first session. It came to him as an epiphany as he was beginning to leave. He said, "Hey, that might be it. I think everything started after that."

The entire first session was devoted to a description of his night sweats, his work as an attorney, his relationship with his law firm partners, and also about his relationship with his wife, whom he claimed he adored, despite their "different personalities." His insight at the end of that first session contained the substantive material out of which, in the second session, emerged the stuff of the symptom. Yet, in that initial first session, his narrative was characterized by complaints. He didn't like one of his partners, and since his was a so-called boutique firm with only eight lawyers (four of whom were partners), having difficulties with one partner was a problem.

Further, he said that his wife was beautiful and that he had never stopped being in love with her even though it was hard for him to get her to do anything he wanted. They attended the cultural events that she chose, went to various other events also, he thought, that she was more interested in than he, and vacationed where she wanted to vacation. He also admitted that he didn't really care about these kinds of decisions and usually left things to her.

The profile of their relationship that emerged during the first session was one in which a rather successful but really passive, submissive, and deferent man, was married to an assertive and willful woman and that as the years passed, the tradition that had developed in their relationship consisted, on his part, of an ineffectiveness, and on her part, on an insistence on having things the way she wanted them. The onus, however, was on both of them. It seemed the wife was, according to him, willful, stubborn, unreasonable, and overentitled. Yet he himself, was in collusion. He made no real effort at asserting himself generally, or even specifically, of asserting any particular entitlements that he may have felt. Thus, the picture of their relationship, in the sense of a metaphor, was one in which he would probably have had to *sweat* bullets to get anything he wanted. Better yet, he probably felt there would be no chance of igniting any real striving for something he wanted, so the sweating of bullets would then, necessarily, have had to be done symbolically.

This man's epiphany at the end of the first session regarding his suggestion of starting a family, and its relation to the onset of his sweating symptom, as well as his description in the second session of his relationship to his wife, revealed that he felt that any further discussion of having a child with her would be met with an automatic, even tacit dismissal. His desire to discuss this issue with her, especially since his was of a secondary status in their relationship, meant that he could not be quite direct enough in impressing her with what he wanted. Moreover, his apparent trepidation in the relationship also may have meant that he himself probably wasn't even sure that he really wanted to have a baby, even though, in fact, he really may have wanted one. The point is that presumably, and in effect, he may have felt so diminished in the relationship that to really want something without his wife's approval probably could not be brought to consciousness by him in any vivid or crystallized way. In addition, it seemed that he was operating with a large measure of denial. For example, no matter how much he complained about her intractability, he maintained that he loved her nevertheless. His denial was not so much related to the veracity of his love for her as it was directed to the avoidance of a self-awareness regarding strong negative feelings toward her that might be present, coexisting with his love for her.

However, in short order, it became evident to him that he really did want a child. Apparently, he and his wife had several quick interactions about this subject, all of them ending with his wife abruptly exiting the discussion. He then broached the subject with her in a more direct manner, which she rejected out of hand. "I'm not having a baby, period," is how he reported she said it. There was no further discussion. She indicated she had never been keen on having children, and that attitude and feeling had not changed. She wasn't sure it would ever change. No matter what he said, the answer was the same. It was then that he felt entirely silenced and rejected.

It now seemed that the specific stimulus in the formation of the symptom was this exchange about having/not having a child. This interaction preceded the appearance of his night sweats, and was most certainly the pivotal event that set off the psychological-emotional process leading to the manifestation of his night sweats symptom.

Applying the Symptom-Code

With respect to the symptom-code, it was clear that the *who* with whom he was angry, was his wife. The fact that he could not access his anger toward her seems to support the assumption that anger was indeed present in this man, but that the anger was repressed.

With respect to the *wish,* his sense of rejection implied that his wish was for his wife to change her mind and not reject him; that is, his wish would be considered an indirect one, a wish for him to avoid something, to avoid rejection. Thus, because it was such an indirect avoidant wish (to avoid rejection), then it could be predicted that the symptom would be one that sustained or increased his discomfort. The night sweats were terribly inconvenient, uncomfortable, embarrassing, and all encompassing as well, leaving him somewhat disoriented and in a sleepy state, ultimately making him feel regressed.

In the final analysis, the symptom was the wish gratified, albeit in neurotic or perverse form, because in order to possibly get what he wanted – a child – he had to *sweat*.

Understanding the Symptom

As a case in which the subject was rejected, the symptom of night sweats was a direct link to what this man really wished for. At first, his description of his wife sounded as though she was an angel. Yet, a more detailed history revealed that there was much under the surface, and outside of his awareness, suggesting a more complicated story.

The onset of the symptom was an acute one and there was no history of any chronic symptom in his personality even remotely resembling this highly idiosyncratic one of night sweats. There was also an absence in his history of any severely somatized symptoms, and no evidence of any psychotically entrenched symptom, or of any delusional thinking. Although his symptom of night sweats was indeed an accessible one, subject to psychotherapy, nevertheless it was one that sustained his discomfort and his tension, because essentially, his wish was for his wife to become less intractable and more reasonable so that perhaps he might be able to then have his wish realized of having a child. In this sense the wish was for his wife to shift her disavowals regarding having children. Because of this indirect targeted wish, his symptom of night-sweats caused him embarrassment and psychological and emotional distress.

With progressive sessions, it became evident that it was not some minor or even parenthetical urge he had to become a father. In fact, he confessed he had been wanting a child for a while but had only recently broached the subject with his wife, and correspondingly, been rebuffed by her. It was this experience of rejection, along with his belief that he was helpless in the face of her refusals, that ultimately led to his repression of anger or even rage. Therefore, the extent of his unconscious anger toward her, seemed to have produced a rather exaggerated symptom in which, hypothetically, he may have been symbolically matching the extent of her stubbornness and refusals, by an equal amount of effort in this highly symbolic act of doing something that would get him his true wish–a baby; he was sweating for what he wanted.

A Case of Obsessive Thoughts of Death

A woman in her late 60's had been consistently diagnosed by various clinicians, over a half century, as a hysteric. She was extremely sensitive to stimuli of various kinds and had what is psychoanalytically known as a thin stimulus barrier. For example, she was overly sensitive to any kind of medication, and could feel ill at the slightest ingestion of any new medicinal agent. Consistent with this hysterical style, taking medical tests was anathema to her because the anticipation of such tests could throw her into a panic. Any suggestion of an invasive procedure of any kind would prove to be extraordinarily aversive to her and she would effectively neutralize all such attempts with the maximum protest. She would simply refuse to accede to the doctor's request for whatever test was called for.

She was, by her own definition, "spiritual," and would consult with all kinds of crystal ball gazers, self-appointed gurus, and various and sundry unconventional, so-called alternative types of self-proclaimed treatment personnel, like-minded spirits and "specialists." In addition, and ironically, despite her resistance to conventional medical attention, she was hypochondriacal and so would habitually visit conventional medical specialists, only to then resist their treatment suggestions.

She was a large woman, quite overweight, and given to passivity; that is, she would want everyone to do for her, often claiming fatigue and nausea. She was widowed, but her two adult sons were always trying to accommodate her, and would provide her with housekeepers, cooks, and even chauffeurs, to drive her here and there, especially to her doctors' appointments. No matter how much was done for her, she would consistently complain, whining that things were terrible. The only arena in which her passivity was absent, was at her place of business, a physical therapy practice. She was part owner, and apparently this status had given her a great sense of empowerment.

Despite her obesity, she was constantly eating sweets, and her diet consisted of anything she fancied. Finally, in the recent past, immediately before she initiated psychotherapy treatment, she began having intrusive and terrifyingly obsessive thoughts about dying. In each and every conversation she would have with family members or friends, she would steer the conversation to the issue of death.

It was these death thoughts that created terrible anxiety in her and drove her to seek psychotherapeutic help. The first thing she said in the very first session was: "Do you have them too?" What she wanted to know was whether the therapist also had such death thoughts, as though she couldn't imagine anyone not having such thoughts. However, in her case, such thoughts were obsessive and she claimed she thought them many times each day until she felt consumed by them.

"Isn't it terrible," she said, wide-eyed. "Doesn't it bother you that everyone dies?"

The Initial Consultation

She began with information about her late husband who had died 10 years earlier at the age of 80. He was more than 20 years her senior and apparently had always been devoted to her. When they married, she was not quite 19, and he was about 40. He died suddenly of a heart attack one week after they celebrated their 40th anniversary.

Her husband was the co-owner of a large physical therapy practice. She first met him when she was 17. He had hired her part-time with an official job title of assistant secretary. She was thrilled to have the job and was grateful to him for hiring her. The job consisted of general office work, some filing, and running errands.

According to the patient, he became friendly with her soon after she began work-ing there. It didn't take very long before this friendliness evolved into a mentoring situation, which developed quite naturally because the patient had lost both parents in a plane crash about three years earlier, when she was 14. She was then very much in need of a parent figure, especially since she was quite a dependent person. After the passing of her parents, she moved in with an older married sister who was busy raising a family The patient felt lost and proclaimed: "My husband rescued me."

After her husband died, she began to experience intermittent bouts of "depres-sion and fears," but the support of her two sons seemed to stem the tide of any psychopathological momentum. Occasionally, over the past 10 years, she would think of death and would, as she put it, "get a shiver." But this "shiver" experience was fleeting. It was only in the recent past, preceding the first consultation, that she began to obsess about death, and for the first time, she was not able to avoid the thought. She was now vulnerable to a state of "shiver," much of the time.

She also stepped into her late husband's role as co-owner of the business, and the partner in the business ostensibly welcomed her presence. Naturally, the part-ner was the clinical professional in the business, and the patient was responsible for the administrative end. This seemed to work well for some years. Yet, some-how over the past year, the practice began to dwindle, until their patient census was so low that the business could no longer justify its existence, and it was agreed by both of them to finally terminate the partnership and the business. The partner took the remaining patients into his own physical therapy private practice agreeing that over a certain period of time, she would share in a portion of the fees yielded by these patients.

This agreement worked smoothly until she discovered, that unbeknownst to her, this partner had been siphoning patients throughout the year, and most likely, over all of the time since her husband's death. As a result, the partner had devel-oped a thriving practice elsewhere. She began to experience the obsession with death almost immediately following this revelation.

Applying the Symptom-Code

It seemed that what kept this large, rather sturdy woman with the fragile ego intact, was the sense of empowerment she enjoyed from her position as co-owner of her late husband's physical therapy practice. It was the only place where she felt whole. Otherwise, she was complaining, passive, and dependent, and gener-ally displayed a rather sour disposition.

After her husband's death, she began to intermittently experience fears of her own death. It then also became evident that the death of her business, along with her sense of profound sudden disempowerment regarding what she called "being fleeced," as well as her helplessness with respect to gaining some rectification, and even restitution, rather than producing a flattening of affect and depression, instead generated an agitated state of obsession with her own demise, her own death as the thematic centerpiece of this obsession. In addition, it would not be far-fetched to assume that she really was wishing for the death of her former partner.

Because her symptom was so obviously related to this recent traumatic event of her disempowerment, the obsessive death fear was highly likely to be an accessible symptom–one that would yield to psychotherapy through the application of the symptom-code. For one, her anger toward this former business partner was palpable, and it was easy to see that he was the *who*. Two, even though it was obvious to her that she was furious with him, nevertheless the extent and depth of her sense of disempowerment, and the profound helplessness accompanying it, could not help but generate a considerable rage reaction, much of which was probably repressed. Once the rage was repressed, the symptom of the intrusive obsessive thought of death became a logical product of her psyche.

So what wish did the death obsession, the symptom, gratify? The answer to this question lay in the issue of the death of her husband, the death of her business, and her presumed wish for the death of this partner. However, her basic wish, the most immediate one, focused on avoiding something. This "something" she apparently wanted to avoid was the thought that she had been undermined and rendered helpless. It was a thought that she found so painful that it became impossible for her to specifically focus, no less dwell on it.

Finally, the astounding psychological fact seemed to be that what she really wished for, was her own death. Symbolically speaking, being dead would mean she was not compelled to look at, think about, or experience the worst possible thought, that of complete disempowerment, and therefore, of nothingness, of a fractured life and a fractured self-esteem. Since the wish was an indirect (avoidant) one, then the obsessive death symptom produced an increase and not a relief of tension.

Understanding the Symptom

The basic principle underlying the assumption that she wished for her own death, and that this wish underpinned her obsessive focus on, and extreme fear of death, lies in the discovery made by Freud. It was a discovery of major significance in the understanding of the operation of the psyche, its logic, and its products–its manifestations. Freud said that behind the fear is the wish. In this case, the wish was to avoid the pain of her dreadful situation – to be dead is to avoid the pain. Thus, again, according to Freud, no wish will be denied, and so the symptom is the wish gratified, albeit in neurotic or perverse form.

To continue in this psychoanalytic frame, her husband's death also qualified as an event that disempowered her, and for all intents and purposes, generated rage against him as well, especially because of his unfair treatment of her by his dying–and, in addition, by dying so suddenly, without preparing her, without warning her. In the psyche, where logic is influenced as much by the rules of needs, and by the personality of basic emotions, as much as it is by reason and the rules of civilization, she, whether rightly or wrongly, almost certainly felt abandoned by him–death or no death. Her reaction to this abandonment had more to do with needs and emotions than it did with reason or logic.

In a dependent person, and especially in this woman, who had been so sheltered by her husband, this sort of sudden death would, of course, usually be experienced not only as an abandonment, but more specifically, as an oedipal abandonment. In fact, such an unexpected sudden death, especially of an oedipal figure, can be experienced as emotionally equivalent to a homicidal act. And in this case, so far as she was concerned, the homicidal act could be understood as having been perpetrated by her husband with her as the victim. In this sense she must have been furious with him, repressed the anger, and had the first of her bouts with obsessional death thoughts. What saved her then, when her husband died, was the structure offered her by the business, and the opportunity to be productive in it. Apparently, that's what stemmed the flow of the potentially chaotic reaction in her psyche that could have easily prevailed were it not also for the presence of her husband's partner, who provided her with a surrogate oedipal figure, that in all likelihood calmed her raging unconscious.

Her immediate problem was that she was spending far too much time behind *The Line* in withdrawal fantasies. With a further integration of the dynamics of the symptom-code, the fear-of-death symptom would be more accessible to cure.

Chapter 8
Gazing at Corpses:
A Case of Morbid Compulsion

A 29-year-old physician, in order to view corpses that were in various stages of dissection, began to obsess about visiting the pathology department of the medical school/hospital to which he was affiliated. He would fix on this usually after working hours, when his shift at the hospital was completed.

The thought of making this sort of "visit," began rather as an idea. "It came from nowhere," he said. Apparently, it felt almost incidental. "At the beginning, it was only a thought," he said. Then the idea began to insinuate itself into his consciousness as an intrusive thought, occupying more than just an incidental moment in his overall stream of consciousness.

After a while, the intrusive nature of the thought reached the point where the patient finally diagnosed himself as "being possessed." Of course, what he meant was that the intrusive thought felt to him as though it was put into him. About viewing these corpses, he said, "It was obviously weird – I actually wanted to look at, or really, gaze at, dead bodies." Then this "possession" began to cause him tension. The tension increased with time as he increasingly felt that he actually needed to see the bodies. He also noticed that whenever he actually viewed the corpses, his tension abated. Thus, the intrusive thought caused him tension, but acting on his compulsion enabled him to relieve the tension.

When he first began visiting the pathology department, he felt relieved gazing at the corpses. However, he knew that his behavior was, as he put it, "sick." It was this idea of it being sick, and his realization that he was in the grip of a complete compulsive symptom, that eventually led him into treatment.

This person had been at this medical school/hospital for the past two years as a staff physician in cardiology. He reported that, at this time, his wife had noticed that he was beginning to seem removed, detached. She would ask him what he was thinking about, and his answer was the standard, "nothing." It was only after two or three months that he slipped with the information that he was spending time after work in the pathology department, at which point his wife wanted to know what he was doing there. Then he confessed that he was body watching, looking at corpses. He told her he couldn't help it and that he knew there was something wrong but didn't have the slightest idea what it was that was wrong. She became alarmed, they discussed it, and he came for treatment.

The Initial Consultation

"I gaze at them." That was his first reference to looking at the corpses. "And I don't know why. It's a mystery. I know it's a symptom." In short order, he described his life and his work, and based upon his body- watching impulse, diagnosed himself as having a morbid compulsion. The diagnosis was accurate. Further, he said that when he had the thought of wanting to go and view the corpses, but for whatever reason was unable to, he then felt an increase in tension. The tension would last, and would be the energy that fueled his inability to stop thinking about it. The only way for him to feel relieved was to get to the pathology department and look at the bodies.

In this first consultation, and in a cursory manner, he focused on his childhood. He indicated that, throughout his childhood his family was encouraging and affectionate with him. He then described the history of his courtship and marriage, then his medical school experiences as a student, and chronologically from there, his internship, and finally his residency. He described friendships and professional relationships, and expressed consternation at not being able to understand what had happened to him to develop such an obviously disturbed clinical symptom. He claimed never before to have had any symptoms that could remotely even be said to be psychological. Yet, he felt this morbid body watching was entirely psychological.

He said that he and his wife discussed it each night when he returned home because, after work, before he would leave for home he almost always made a first stop at the pathology department. His wife had begun to feel that he was overworked and that the symptom may have represented his feeling that he was "dying" from fatigue. Hence, his gazing at dead bodies would be an identification with being dead because of working so hard. According to the patient, his wife had taken some psychology courses and had a theory about the psychology of identification, as well as mentoring or modeling behavior, which according to him, she applied to almost any problem.

The patient dismissed his wife's theory largely because he did not agree with her assessment that he was overworked. The truth was, he said, that he felt underutilized in his hospital department, so he was not feeling at all overworked. He also said that at times he would get "a fright" that maybe he had some unconscious impulse toward necrophilia, but then again denied ever feeling erotic toward the corpses. He said, "I know, at least consciously, that I have no sexual feelings about the bodies whatsoever. It's not that. I'm pretty sure it's not that."

Finally, before the end of the initial session, he began to discuss his current job responsibilities. To the question, "In what respect do you feel underutilized?" he easily answered, "The chief of service just doesn't use me enough." This led to a discussion of his relationship with the chief of service, who, as it turned out, he was at odds with.

The chief of service had been ambivalent about hiring him in the first place, but the doctor-applicant the chief of service chose selected another hospital, so that the chief then settled on the patient as a second choice. Somehow this information had gotten back to the patient and he began feeling awkward when in the chief's presence.

The patient also noticed that this chief of service was assigning duties to other, less experienced members of his staff, while omitting the patient from some of the more interesting assignments. A somewhat acrimonious confrontation about this presumed slight by the chief ensued, and in the end, the chief denied the patient's allegation of neglect.

The patient said that the chief "didn't have the guts to just call a spade a spade." The patient felt that it had been since then that "a cold relationship" had developed between them, and the patient, in addition to feeling underutilized, began really to feel ignored.

It was not possible to pin down precisely whether the friction between the chief and the patient correlated to the onset of the patient's symptom, but it seemed that such an unpleasant work situation would certainly have involved, or even challenged, the patient's identity as a physician, and also very likely raised issues of competence, and professional respect.

Applying the Symptom-Code

In this case, the symptom had an acute onset in a person who had never before complained of any kind of psychological disturbance. Hence, there was no reported history of chronic embeddedness of the symptom in his personality. His health was excellent and there was no reason to assume that he had developed any kind of chemical change that would cause a paranoid or morbid compulsion to specifically gaze at bodies. The fact was that there was nothing he wanted to do with the bodies but look at them.

In view of this particular onset-pattern, the symptom would have to be considered an accessible one with respect to psychotherapy, with the prediction of a complete and efficient cure. Of course the questions to answer were: What was his *wish*? and who was the *who*? The assumption was also accepted that he was angry at this *who* and finally, that the anger toward that person was repressed.

It soon became evident that he was terribly put off by what he considered a very transparent ostracism by this chief of service, who now became a chief suspect in the search for the *who*. His wife was not a good choice for the original object of his anger because their relationship seemed to be on solid ground, and he felt that his wife was, and had always been, a great support for him. A review of the remaining cast of characters in his life was fundamentally benign. It was both by default as well as by an objective look at the people in his life that the choice for the *who* was reduced to one person–the chief of service.

Thus, the stage was set to analyze the symptom by considering the chief of service as the original object of his anger. The remaining task was to identify his basic wish. It seemed that the wish would have been some hope, even desperate hope, that the *who*, the chief, would resolve his dissatisfaction toward the patient and treat him as he did all the other professional staff.

Understanding the Symptom

It also seemed that the key to understanding the meaning of the symptom lay in the patient's relationship within his nuclear family. For example, in his childhood he felt entirely legitimate and loved. At the hospital–his professional family–the chief of service, symbolically also a parent figure, and who could for many, be a nurturer, someone who encouraged participation, and offered support and reassurance, was for the patient, someone to consciously fear and perhaps, even unconsciously hate. As a child, at home, he indeed achieved his aim of gratifying his wishes for love and attention. However at the hospital, he was not at all able to achieve this aim. And since he had little or no experience with rejection, now he was apparently unable to manage it well.

It was a good bet that the patient was essentially angry with the chief, especially because he felt he could not be empowered or have any influence whatsoever in the department, so long as the chief was in charge. Disempowerment was the patient's strongest conscious feeling. If this was the case, then he would have been instantly furious as a way to reempower himself. However, it seems obvious that he was not able to express the rage directly. The assumed repression of the anger, therefore would naturally produce a symptom that in its symbolic form represented the gratification of the wish; that is, with the chief of service dead, then at least the patient's sense of rejection would be nullified.

This interpretation was made in the session and the patient instantly recognized the truth of it, that he wanted the chief of service dead. He was so angry at this chief that he acted the anger out by urgently needing to look at dead bodies. He was really acting out his wish that whenever he went to the pathology department, the body he would see, would be that of the chief. So he constructed an elaborate and seemingly bizarre scenario in which he got the chief to be dead symbolically, and so felt much better when he viewed the corpses.

After examining the meaning of the symptom, the patient felt that something had changed and that the entire ritual now had a different meaning. Of course, what he meant was that the whole thing was no longer unconscious. As an unconscious ritual it had one meaning and created a corresponding mysterious mood. On a conscious level, however, the mysterious mood was absent and the meaning was different because there was no longer a need to act out something without knowing what it was. The patient no longer felt possessed. In addition, he was sure that his morbid compulsion to gaze at dead bodies could no longer have a grip on him.

After a while his relationship to his chief of service also evolved and the patient felt no longer either afraid or angry at this person. Apparently, because of a change in the patient's attitude to this chief of service, both the patient and the chief began to react more favorably to one another.

Of course whenever he acted out the body watching, his direct wish for the chief to be dead relieved his tension. His new attitude toward the chief also moved him from a behind *The Line* position into one of "doing," in front of *The Line*.

Chapter 9
Sin of the Priest: A Case of Obsession

"It's a good thing that thinking something and doing something are two different things. Otherwise you could call my case, 'The Sin of the Priest.' But, thank God," he continued, "it's all on the level of fantasy."

This was the first remark made by a 70-year-old male priest after he introduced himself at the very first session. He was a portly man with a big stomach and an affable and easy manner. He was intelligent, erudite, and psychologically minded. It was strikingly clear that he was not at all shy about relating the events that encouraged him to seek treatment.

It relieved him to say that he was perhaps close to sinning but had not really sinned. It was not that any act of his was, according to his own standards, sinful. Rather, at first, it was not clear whether or not he actually believed his stated certainty that he had not sinned. In other words, the question was: Did he or didn't he?

The Initial Consultation

A review of his recent therapy history was how he introduced his intrusive thought. Apparently, his former therapist was the one to identify his thought as intrusive. He had seen this therapist for a short period of time in an attempt to rid himself of this intrusive thought that had become an incessant preoccupation. But the treatment had not affected the symptom at all, and after a while, he discontinued his sessions.

The thought involved a woman parishioner who had been a member of his congregation beginning some years earlier. He said, "When I first saw her, I was instantly smitten." At that time, he was in his mid-60's and she, in her 30's. "Now she's probably about 35, and I'm 70," he continued. His focus on the difference in their ages was also a factor in his difficulty in thinking about this woman. He indicated that she was beautiful and that he had always been, and was still now, beguiled by her. He also said that his ideas about her had been torturing him for years, and that it was these ideas that had intruded into his psyche, into his consciousness, and like a song that can obsessively haunt a person, this intrusive thought was every bit as relentless.

One of his fantasies regarding this woman was that he would leave the church and marry her. He claimed she was the only person in his priestly existence who had ever had this sort of effect on him, and that because of his obsession with her, and especially because of his intrusive thought, he also felt that his personal dignity was compromised. Thus, his embarrassment was with himself alone. As it turned out, the intrusive thought was actually more than a thought, it was a rhapsody!

Over the years, he and this parishioner had gotten to know one another and although they had often chatted, and even worked together on a church project, she had never approached him either for advice or confession or for any other kind of non-church contact. In addition, he said she had never flirted with him or otherwise indicated that sort of interest. However, she would unfailingly, always express appreciation whenever he would reflect back to her what he considered to be her positive attributes, and he was sure she knew that he admired her. In this respect he admitted that it was he, who both in oblique ways, and sometimes in a studied, although tentative manner, was the one who flirted. However, he did it indirectly, and with hoped-for subtlety, so that it was more like an autistic communication about which, probably, only he would be aware. Thus, he felt he was involved in a one-sided love affair.

When these so-called autistic trysts occurred, he would think to himself: "What am I doing? This is insanity." Yet, he was in an inexorable thrall with respect to the feeling he had for her. He felt less in her actual grip and more in his own—where everything about this situation turned in on him. He then also indicated that about the time the intrusive thought crystallized, he had become gluttonous, and because of this unusual appetite, gained 40 pounds over the period of the past several years, equal to the life-span of his intrusive thought symptom.

He then described the symptom itself by introducing it with what to him was a terribly dispiriting story. He said that three years earlier, this woman had married a fellow parishioner. He quickly went on to say that, at present they had no children. It was possible that he quickly added the information about her childless marriage because in that way he could possibly keep her virginal. He also admitted to not being able to bear the thought that she would be in any conjugal relationship with anyone else. So far as he was concerned, she was saint like, and entirely, as he said, "unsullied." He was able, at times, to make himself believe that her marriage was strictly for companionship and asexual. He then admitted to feeling that this was nonsense, so that at other times he would try to imagine what her face looked like in ecstasy, and would then try to visualize her expression during what he imagined to be her orgasm. When his thoughts took this turn, he said he felt himself "sink into nothingness," and he had great difficulty coming out of, what he then considered to be "a despair."

He introduced the intrusive thought by saying: "Some time after she married, I noticed I was having this strange thought."

The Intrusive Thought

"In the thought, in the fantasy, she tells me that she has scores and scores of cysts and little sores like pimples, that get popped and extrude pus. They're all on her back and they look like little craters; red around the edges with pus accumulating at the head. She tells me they are painful and that she cannot permit any doctor to puncture them because the slightest pressure on her back can cause severe pain. Well, no, not exactly. I think what it is in the fantasy is that she says she hasn't found the doctor with the right touch. Yes, that's it. It's not that the doctors can't do it. It's that the doctors can't do it in a way that avoids pain. She says the pressure on each of the cysts has to be just right, and in my thoughts I get the impression that it is I, who will be the one able to put exactly the right amount of pressure to each cyst on her back, because I'm so in need of her, I so empathize with her, that I can sense exactly what it is that she needs.

"And so we're in her bathroom or in her bedroom-it changes in my mind from time to time-and I'm not sure how it transpires, but I begin to persuade her to let me try. I just begin to try and she permits me. And then different things happen. For one, there's a scene where she is partially disrobed but holding her blouse or sweater against her breasts. I tell her that that's not important now because we're concentrating on more important things. So, she drops the clothing and leans over. I see her breasts. They are modest, but merely seeing them is not what makes me happy. Because it's not about sex at this point. It's about my happiness in helping her and in her permitting me to get this close and intimate with her. It's about spending time together. She's giving me her time and sharing with me–and only with me–her most personal concern. And when I've helped her and broken all the cysts and thus when I'm successful with her, we then get even more intimate, but still not sexual, and in my fantasy, I then run a hot tub and gently lower her into it. You see, she has to soak so the cysts will continue to drain. The cysts are full of pus and they keep draining. And because of that she's in my hands and we need to be together, working on this problem and curing her, purifying her, emptying her of all that pus. And then the fantasy switches to another variation of the theme because the intimacy has been satisfied. But now something more, or even more important needs to be satisfied.

"What I do in this next version, is make a template of the scores of cysts and pus- sores on her back. At first the template is on paper which I've placed on her back in order to trace the exact location of the sores and cysts. Then I somehow transfer the paper template to a large board that now contains the exact map of the sores and cysts on her back, both with respect to size and circumference of each as well as the distance of one from the other. If you place the template-board on her back, all the sores will peek through their respective holes on the template. Then in the fantasy, I place her on what could be a massage table, and the template board for her back is the surface upon which she lies, so when she lies down, all the cysts and sore-like pimples will fit directly into their respective holes. Then as she lies on her back on the table, the weight of her body pressing down begins to naturally cause the array of eruptions through the holes. Under the template are balloons attached to each hole so that when pus drains from each site, the pus then collects into its own cyst balloon. None of it is wasted. Not a drop. It's all collected.

"Then when that's done, I sometimes have her soak in the tub for a time while I stand at the tub and watch her soak. I'm slightly bowed looking at her and we're talking. And she is naked in the tub. And she is becoming accustomed to me seeing her in her nakedness. And the fact that she becomes accustomed to me seeing her like this is also very satisfying. It means that she is relaxed with me even though she is naked. Therefore she is more intimate with me than with anyone else. Oh yes, I also pop the cysts with my hands and I wear rubber gloves in the fantasy. I'm never doing it with bare hands. Then I have her stand, and I go to work again because after soaking in this hot bath, more pus has collected, and then I finally push the rest out by pressing my fingers against each cyst. This time even more pus is emitted and the final amount gushes out of each cyst giving her tremendous relief as if pounds of weight have been lifted. Then, out of sheer love for me, she falls asleep naked in my arms, in bed. This part of the fantasy then fades, as though I'm spent. It's not like an orgasm or a sexual feeling, but it's a feeling of relief and a satisfaction that I get. At that point I no longer need to continue the fantasy. I find that I then go about my normal life until another time, when the fantasy returns and I go through the same thing again. And it happens all the time. And that's it. But it's not it, because, believe it or not, I'm celibate and that's how it has always been. I've never had a sexual relationship."

He then indicated that he hadn't seen this woman in the past year but had heard from others, who had seen her. After he heard that she was in touch with others in the parish, he related the following:

"Since then, I started to think of actually having sex with her. I broke through a barrier there. It's the typical missionary position and we are in passionate sex. I can see her face is quite sexual and her expression is that of a woman in the throes of an orgasm. This is when I feel she's mine."

After relating this new development regarding the fantasy of actual sex with this woman he indicated that at that point in the fantasy, the intrusive thought, or the intrusive scenario, was getting the best of him and that it really was out of control. He was thinking about it all the time.

"I think about it every day, even several times a day. It's obsessive. I can't figure out when it will appear or why. Now it has me worried more than ever. And even more than the sex–I can understand the sexual part–but why am I thinking about cysts and pus?"

He also then repeated that it was after she married that he gained all his extra weight, and he remembered a dream. He said, "All I remember of the dream is a fragment. She said to me, 'Well, you just have a hunger for me.' " And I awakened. Now I know it means just that–I have a hunger for her. The fact is I've gained more than 40 pounds over a three year period. My appetite knows no bounds. And she married three years ago also. At 5 feet 9 inches, I usually weighed 165 pounds. Now I'm 230. I look at myself and I'm horrified."

Applying the Symptom-Code

Although the symptom and its embeddedness in an elaborate fantasy seems fantastical, nevertheless the symptom itself is bound by the three constituents of the symptom-code: the *wish*; *repressed anger;* and the *who*. These are the components of the code, that when applied, will reveal the meaning of the symbols and action of the fantasy–actually reveal the meaning of this patient's magnificent obsession, this rhapsody, which had so tortured him.

The important questions were: (1) what was his basic wish; (2) who was the *who* toward whom he was angry; and (3) why was the anger repressed? It was predicted that once these questions could be answered, and once he did something related to the original problem, at that point the symptom would be severely challenged, and might be entirely eliminated from his experience, from his life.

The *who* seemed to be the best place to start. Since he was so fixed on this woman, and could not focus on anything or anyone else, it seemed that to first consider her as the *who* toward whom he was basically angry, would be a good bet. Yes, despite his avowed love for, and esteem of this woman, the hypothesis that seemed most valid, was that given his symptom he was probably *angry* or even furious at her–unconscious though these feelings may have been. Of course he would not at all be in touch with such feelings, especially because he was so enthralled with her.

Thus, the identification of this woman as the *who* was a reasonable guess, and the *repression of anger* toward her, was also assumed as a given. The *wish* remained as the psychological key to the entire symptom problem. What then could the wish have been? Actually, this was not really a mystery.

His wish, of course, was for her to love him. It was as simple as that. Certainly, on top, more or less consciously, he wanted her to love him. Under it, however, because she didn't respond in kind, then he felt his wish to have been frustrated, unrequited, thwarted. And it was a terrible feeling of disempowerment for him, if only because his wish was so very strong, so very intense. This was the respect in which he felt disempowered, and the natural reflex of anger could not be acknowledged consciously. Therefore, his only alternative was to repress the anger. The anger was then directed at the self and since the wish also was represented in the unconscious, then presumably he at once developed the symptom of the intrusive thought–the scenario of cysts and so forth.

Apparently, his wish was gratified by the expressing of pus, an important point. In his fantasy, she permits him to accomplish his aim, and then he feels relieved. She gives him access to her naked body, but that is not the central point, though it is a contributing factor in his gratification through the symptom. In fact, in describing his elaborate fantasy, he emphasized that his true and complete relief only came when his aim was accomplished –when he finally got all the pus out.

Applying the symptom-code reveals first that his *wish* was for her to love him, to give to him. Second, this also means that she was the *who*. Third, by deduction, when his wish was thwarted, he became angry at her and then *repressed the anger*. What remained was the meaning of the symptom and its relation to his elaborate fantasy.

Understanding the Symptom

Of course there are symbols throughout the fantasy, but the focus here will be to target only the spine of the fantasy and not any secondary considerations. What has already been implied, teased out here, is that he was angry at her but that also his wish was indeed satisfied, albeit in perverse form, by way of the symptom. The symptom was really symbolized by getting pus out and saving every drop of it in balloons. Everything else, including tracing the cysts on her back and making a template was done in the fantasy only so the crescendo of getting the pus out and saving every drop, would be reached. It was only then that he felt truly satisfied. Even though her trust in him was a source of solace, for example, in her acceptance of him standing by the tub watching her soak, nevertheless this was not the sine qua non or essence of the symbolic gratification of his wish. It was close, but not yet a fully flowered and fully satisfied aim. That true aim was accomplished with the extrusion, draining, and collecting of the pus to the very last drop.

To understand the symptom, the extruding pus collected to the last drop needed to be related to this wish for her to love him. This was the key to the entire symbolic nature of his elaborate fantasy construction—to connect the wish with the extrusion of pus—which in a short-hand way, resulted in a symptom called an intrusive thought.

Since the wish was for her to love and to give to him, the question became, what is one process through which a woman gives? What is one way a woman can give both symbolically as well as actually? She deprived him, but deprived him of what? The answer with respect to an analogy may lie in the psychoanalytic understanding of the language of dreams. For example, in dreams sometimes things are backwards or opposite. Up can mean down, in can mean out, young can mean old; so too with symptoms. Thus, the law of opposites can apply in symptoms as well as in dreams. And just as the law of opposites in dreams presumably disguises the true meaning of the dream, so too does this same law act to disguise the meaning of the symptom in the overall sense, as well as the meaning, specifically of the wish.

Therefore, in this person's fantasy, with respect to the drama unfolding on the woman's back, it may be highly likely that the real drama was on the woman's front—the opposite of her back. Thus, all the pimples or sores or cysts on her back were really on her front. What do such configurations look like? Well, in his fantasy he described the cysts as crater-like and red, and that they had a head to them where the pus accumulated.

When confronted with this picture of the front rather than the back, as well as his original rendition of how the pimples and sores looked, the patient practically shouted, "It's nipples. It's nipples. I'm thinking about her breasts. That's what it's all about."

He was right. He was thinking about her breasts, and the focus on her back was a psychological shift, a disguise. The question now became why was he thinking about her breasts? And apparently the answer was concealed in his feeling that he was being deprived; that is, even though she liked him, and was friendly with him, nevertheless, she never demonstrated anything other than that. This left him feeling unrequited. His wish was that she be giving to him and that meant symbolically, that her breasts would give milk. And this explains why he needed to collect every drop of the pus–because the pus was a most ingenious disguise for the milk. Since every drop presumably represented her milk, then in the fantasy, the symbol of the pus, and the importance of collecting it, meant that she was giving everything she had to him–her milk; that is, she was giving him all of her love, concern, nourishment.

Thus, when he got all of the pus out, that's when he felt true and complete relief. Only then did it mean that she gave to him the maximum love and nurturance that she had to give. And she gave it only to him; not to the doctors. In this sense he was right, the entire fantasy was never about sex, it was actually about acceptance. He just wanted to be accepted by her.

Yet, he couldn't have his wish in real life, and so he had the wish in fantasy in the form of a symptom. It was an obsessive-intrusive thought that got a profound grip on him which he couldn't shake. In fact, it was shaking him. And the scores and scores of cysts and pimples on her back represented a multitude of nipples also reflecting the truly desperate nature, as well as magnitude of his yearning and need for her.

So far as his obesity was concerned, this also related to his overwhelming focus on this woman. It could be said that he was eating because he couldn't be without her; that is, he couldn't be empty or alone. To constantly eat, meant never to be alone. In addition to his gluttony, he also stated that in his present life, there was never a time that he didn't feel bloated and this bloated feeling was seen to signify that this woman was always with him. She was the *who*, and since he was presumably so angry with her for depriving him, then he was also really medicating himself with food to assuage the anger, to calm it. In effect, he was actually afraid to be hungry because his empty stomach, his hunger, possibly, would signify that he was without her. Further, he remembered the fragment of his dream in which she said, "Well, you just have a hunger for me." Thus, if he was full, he wouldn't have to know he had a hunger for her. In this sense, the wish to have her was always fulfilled by being full, by being bloated.

It also seemed that he would do anything but admit to himself that he was really angry at her for ignoring him and for leaving him and marrying. He wouldn't and couldn't face this feeling because it would mean that he didn't have her and perhaps never would.

All the symbols involving symptom, cysts, appetite, and stomach, that had so much power over him, had now, in the light of this deciphering increased his consciousness and seemed to have a profound effect on him. It was unlikely that the symptom could ever again become viable. However, in order to fortify the defeat of the symptom, the last task he needed to accomplish was something that related to the relationship that he had had with her. This *doing* activity would bring him in front of *The Line*, and enable him to burn away the inclination to live behind *The Line* in withdrawal where his magnificent obsession/elaborate rhapsodic fantasy lived and thrived, and kept him in a sustained state of high tension.

His answer was that they had worked together on a catalogue for the gifts given to the church but never finished the catalogue because they were working on it at the time she married. She never returned, and he avoided the task of completing the catalogue. Now, perhaps he could get back to it.

But he wasn't finished. He said that not only did he overeat, but he had food cravings, and that these cravings for certain foods was a frequent occurrence. He felt this was a separate symptom even though it may have been related to the entire rumination about this woman. The meaning of his large stomach requires a bit of speculation, the relative validity of which, nevertheless, is based upon an interpretation consistent with the data he provided, and in addition reveals a possible path to understanding this symptom–his large stomach.

The fact was that he had a big stomach on a rather stout frame. He carried his weight well except for this big protruding stomach. He actually looked pregnant, and since there was so much repressed anger directed at his woman friend for her depriving him, then the only way to express a likely interpretation to him, so that both his anger and his attraction to her would be contained in the same word, seemed to be the choice of the colloquial term "fucked." It would seem that he felt fucked by this parishioner. So what happens when you get fucked? You get pregnant! By virtue of this sort of interpretation, it could be construed that his big belly was his pregnancy. Symbolically, he may have been carrying the product of his lady friend's essence in his belly. His gluttony therefore, was his perversion. It too, represented the pleasure he wanted from her but couldn't have, and so he had it another way. And furthermore, perhaps he acted out the pregnancy with food cravings. This can be considered a content-shift, that is, a shift from the internalized object, the woman, to food. In the psyche, as Freud postulated, wishes are never denied. This man wished for her, and in his psyche got his wish.

Symbolically, therefore, being pregnant with her meant that he wouldn't have to face life without her. Of course, in bleak reality, he actually didn't have her. What he had was a fat stomach, and a magnificent obsession.

Chapter 10
Ingenious Regression:
A Case of Hallucination

A woman of 60 had been in an assisted living environment for her entire adult life. Over the years she had consistently scored in the I.Q. range of 65 to 70. Such scores placed her in the category identified as "mild deficiency." In the more antiquated I.Q. language, she would have been classified as retarded.

The mild deficiency designation meant that she could work at a job, especially if her tasks on the job were structured, and if they enabled her to perform in a repetitive and consistent fashion. And indeed, throughout her adult life, she was always employed in one way or another, within the context of a variety of programs that could be defined as "assisted abilities" programs.

This woman had two siblings, a brother and sister, who were never very involved in her life, and would only visit occasionally–a family interest on their part that was perfunctory. Her mother, age 97, was still living and surprisingly, quite active. She was a devoted visitor, and would escort this woman, her 60 year old daughter, home for holidays and for other special occasions.

This mildly deficient woman, was hardly ever ill. In fact, her health was excellent, and she was quite proud of the fact that she had never missed a day of work. Her only identifiable problem was that she was obviously, and severely, dependent on her mother, and would make decisions only with her mother's say so. All of her clothing, and all items and materials she needed, were provided solely by her mother.

Suddenly, at the age of 97, her mother died. She had expired in her sleep. After having been told of her mother's passing, this woman became quickly withdrawn and depressed, and for the first time that anyone could remember, she stopped working.

"Devastating," would be an apt adjective to reflect this woman's state of being after she had been informed of her mother's death. The loss was apparently so profound and her depression so deep, that she stopped eating, and would lie in bed, moaning. She was hospitalized and diagnosed with major depression

Within one day of hospitalization, and even before any plan was made for medication, her depression lifted, and instead, she was floridly hallucinating. She began talking to the air as well as providing dialogue by answer.

The Initial Consultation

During the first consultation, she continued talking to, and answering the air, as well as relating to the examiner, and did it all with relative ease, and in the absence of any depressive mood. She never grimaced or in any other way showed any trace of schizophrenic mentation or behavior. The only exception with respect to psychosis, was the presence of the auditory hallucinations that, it seemed, had entirely usurped her psyche. Her depression was nowhere to be seen.

"He told me I'm 'independent'; he said, 'independent.' And that I shouldn't worry. And that I could take care of myself now. He said he was sure."

This quote was a reference to the psychiatrist who initially conducted the intake interview. Apparently, what had occurred was that in an effort to reassure this patient and to try to be encouraging, the psychiatrist told her that now that her mother was deceased, that he was sure she could handle things herself. This psychiatrist's thinking was that if the patient felt reassured about her abilities then perhaps she would feel less depressed or less lost.

Although the psychiatrist was trying to be supportive–commendable, no doubt–but as it turned out, not insightful. The problem was that the psychiatrist did not at all understand what had happened to the patient. The patient's concern was about her lost object, her mother, upon whom she so depended. She was devastated that her mother was gone. For the patient's entire life, her mother was the person upon whom she was dependent for anything and everything.

Although, in this initial consultation, the various events that had occurred since she learned of her mother's death were reviewed, nothing could explain her dramatic shift, after she was hospitalized, away from depression and into a hallucinatory world. The only intervening and possibly important event seemed to be this exchange between the patient and the intake psychiatrist.

Applying the Symptom-Code

Without the use of the symptom-code to unscramble the mystery of her shift from depression to a psychotic hallucinatory state, it would have been extremely difficult to know where to start. Yet, by applying the symptom-code to this problem, the mystery instantly yielded.

It was assumed that the intake psychiatrist was the *who*. Of course this meant that the patient was angry with him, but that the anger was repressed. In addition, and parenthetically, the assumption was made that perhaps in the unconscious, retardation or even mild deficiency, are not relevant phenomena. Even those people who have lower I.Q. scores still demonstrate conventional psychological symptom formation. This implies that whatever psychodynamics operate to produce psychological-emotional symptoms in people of average or above I.Q.s, must also, by definition, operate with people of below average I.Q.s. Thus, symptom formation, it is proposed, only follows rules of the psyche – and not necessarily solely rules of biology.

Of course, as stated, it was assumed that the patient must have repressed a great amount of anger. This was assumed because a profound shift had taken place in her psyche, most likely concerning the management of this proposed repressed anger. This shift could be characterized as the transformation of a thwarted wish into a hallucinatory symptom. With respect to the structure of the symptom-code, this repressed anger necessarily induced transformation of the thwarted wish into the hallucinatory symptom because, according to the Freudian insight regarding wishes, her wish needed not to be denied. The simple question became, what wish?

In other words, the unconscious process that took place consisted of the transformation of the wish through the repression of anger, into the symptom–in this case a hallucination. The patient's basic wish would necessarily be part of this process insofar as the wish always, and presumably without exception, becomes satisfied as the symptom. Therefore, her hallucination became her gratified wish.

Again, the question remained as to the specific meaning of the wish. What was her wish? The answer was that her wish was simple and actually even obvious.

Understanding the Symptom

It seemed likely that the key to the understanding of the symptom was in the exchange that the intake psychiatrist had with this woman. He told her that now that her mother was gone, she surely was able to take care of herself; that she was a grown up, and could be independent. The problem was that the psychiatrist, despite his good intentions, apparently lacked the insight to see that what this woman wanted most, *what her basic wish was*, was *not* to be independent. She wanted her mother, and she wanted to sustain her life long condition–to be dependent on her mother. Her wish was to have her mother not be dead. Her basic wish, was to have her mother be alive—period; a positive wish.

In a deeper psychoanalytic sense, it could be assumed that because of this woman's life long dependency on her mother, that at an unconscious and deeply repressed level, she harbored resentment toward her mother, and this may have been so, precisely because of her all-consuming dependency on her mother. The ubiquitous principle governing such an assumption is: *dependency breeds rage.* Thus, were it not for the perhaps fortuitous intervention of the psychiatrist, her depression may have given way to other more serious derivatives of depression, namely, chronic despair, or even suicidal implications, from which any remission could be highly doubtful. However, the entire depressive picture shifted to an hallucinatory process culminating in a florid hallucinatory symptom. If, in fact, this was the case, then it could have happened because whatever anger she may have been harboring toward her mother, both as a function of her chronic dependency, as well as because of the abandonment feelings that death confers, may have transferred to the psychiatrist.

It was the intake psychiatrist who very probably became the object of her anger, her *who*. And then this woman who was essentially considered retarded, demonstrated her rather high unconscious I.Q. by proving the psychiatrist wrong.

He said her mother was dead, and that she, the patient, was now independent. But she showed him that she was not at all independent, that she was still dependent, and quite dependent for that matter, on her mother, who now in the hallucination, was very much alive, indeed!

She brought her mother back. And it was a simple regression into a hallucination that did it. She was now floridly hallucinating – that was true. But it was her mother to whom she was talking, and it was her mother who was talking to her. Hence, everything was good with the world. No more depression, no more abandonment, and most importantly, and thankfully, no more independence. The psychiatrist, was wrong on all counts. Dead wrong!

To relinquish the hallucinatory symptom as well as the depression this woman would need to be involved in some *doing* activity related to her work. It would be an attempt to reinforce in front of *The Line* living. For her to understand the wish and the anger also seemed possible, especially as a prelude to the cure of her symptoms.

The rather astonishing result here, is that this I.Q. challenged woman developed a symptom that involved a complex unconscious regressive psychological maneuver. It was a maneuver, nothing short of brilliant, involving a positive wish that generated a shift out of despair and depression, via a hallucination, into emotional relief of tension. Thus, she developed what might be called an ingenious regression, and consequently the symptom of a brilliant hallucination.

Chapter 11
Panic on the Bridge:
A Case of Agoraphobia

An immigrant man of 35 sought treatment because he would become panicky and "break into a sweat," whenever he was driving across a bridge. The immediate effect of this problem concerned a small moving business that he had recently established. He was now transferring people and their possessions from place to place within the city. But he would not accept a job if it required him to drive across a bridge. Although this problem did not make it impossible for his business to succeed, nevertheless, he found himself occasionally turning down work because of it. His problem on the bridge was about the span of the bridge; that is, that it became a problem if the bridge had a distinctly elongated span over water, and therefore, gave him the sense, he said, "like nothing was good, like it was too open." He was also afraid of the water.

On his latest job, apparently he mistook the client's instructions about the destination, and found himself heading onto a bridge which led from one part of the city to the other. There was no way for him to reverse his direction, and because of the congested traffic, he felt it would be embarrassing for him simply to stop. He only made it across because apparently, at some point on the bridge, all traffic slowed to a snail's pace, and his passenger, who became aware of the driver's problem, insisted that they switch seats. The patient was only too glad to do so. Now, the passenger became the driver.

The Initial Consultation

His description of his reactions during this episode made it clear that what he experienced was anxiety and even perhaps panic. As it turned out, this man had been suffering with this symptom for the past five years; according to him, from the time he married. This latest incident of feeling panicked on the bridge when he was the driver, caused him palpitations, and he "broke into a sweat." He described the symptom as one in which he was shaking, and also felt light-headed. It could be assumed, at least from his description of his breathing, that his light-headedness was perhaps a result of what seemed to be also an episode of hyperventilating. His description of his behavior during this traumatic event, temporary though it was, sounded as though he had had a bona fide anxiety or panic attack, which he claimed, "was like the others." He had experienced these symptoms before.

When they had driven over the bridge, rather than continuing on their journey, the new driver exited at his very next opportunity, and retraced their route, taking the patient back over the bridge, and home. As it turned out, the driver was expecting more of the same kind of episode from the patient on the return trip, but the patient explained he only became anxious when he was the driver.

The patient described his therapy experiences of the recent past. He had been treated by two kinds of therapy. The first was strictly a medication regimen consisting of drugs designed to alleviate anxiety and panic. The patient discontinued the use of such medication when it became apparent that his libido was severely affected and as a result, he was less able to feel amorous, or to be sexual. His wife also insisted that the medication was not right for him.

The second round of therapy consisted of a behavioral-cognitive approach in which the therapist attempted to desensitize him to bridges, but with no success whatsoever. From a psychoanalytic point of view, and despite reports of success with such methods, this behavioral-cognitive approach would not at all be considered efficacious, because the problem is not literally about the bridge. Psychoanalytically, the bridge would be considered a symbol, and the main objective would be to try to understand what such a symbol meant.

The patient explained that he came from a large Pakistani Muslim family in which he was the oldest of his siblings, and closest to his mother. He was also the one most eager to stay close to his family. He admitted to being devoted to his mother, but also to loving his wife. He felt that he was persuaded into his marriage by his wife, all the while experiencing great ambivalence.

"I didn't want to hurt her and she wanted to marry me. I did love her, but I didn't feel I could do it yet. I wasn't ready. But I did it."

He admitted to still feeling uncomfortable with his wife in their rather small apartment, although he professed that he did love her and was happily married. They had no children because has he put it, "I don't feel ready yet to have children."

Applying the Symptom-Code

The process, in this present therapeutic situation, was to apply the symptom-code so that he could make conscious that which was presumably unconscious. That is to say, because he was so affected, and even controlled by this symptom, he necessarily must have been harboring repressed anger. It was further assumed that the anger was repressed because he was not able to direct this anger to its intended object—the *who*. Correspondingly, it was the *who*, the person with whom he was angry, who would have been the person to have thwarted his basic *wish*. Thus, the details that needed attention concerned the identity of the *who*, in addition to ascertaining his basic wish.

This man's symptom seemed quite compartmentalized. Although it had been causing him distress, and even interfering, especially with his business life, nevertheless he had kept it isolated, and the symptom itself had apparently never insinuated itself into his amalgam of character traits where it could have usurped the personality. On the contrary, the symptom had remained encapsulated, as it were, within the organization of his personality. The fact was that the symptom was still alien to him despite its five year existence. Thus, it would be expected that on the basis of its alien nature alone, this man's symptom, indeed, would be subject to the talking cure.

It needs to be acknowledged, however, that the more chronic the symptom, the more resistive it becomes to the talking cure. The symptom described here, with respect to its life-span, to its relative longevity has gained some traction and become an iffy proposition, not with respect to cure itself through psychotherapy, but more with respect to efficient cure through psychotherapy. The point is that in this case, with regard to prediction, the issue of cure was not expected to be the crux of the matter. Rather, the issue was expected to be an empirical one. In other words, would the patient respond to the treatment with the use of the symptom-code so that the symptom itself would lift rather quickly, or, because of the relative entrenchment of the symptom, would it turn out to be somewhat more difficult to cure? That was the essential question.

One thing was certain, his problem was not about his fear. Phobia, is never about the fear! In any event, it is almost impossible to reason with the kind of irrational fear that is characterized by a phobia. The real problem was about his repressed anger toward a person who had compromised his wish, and his consequent panic represented his wish realized, albeit in perverse form–the basics of the symptom-code, the *wish*, the *repressed anger*, and the *who*. The coda to the symptom-code, the *doing* – that is, his doing something regarding the original thwarting of his wish, would be the something to decide upon when the unconscious conflict became conscious, and very importantly, if he was able to come to grips with it.

Because of his admitted dependency on his mother, it could be hypothesized that she was the original *who*. But actually he was not very focused on her, and hardly referred to her. He also didn't say very much about his father or about his siblings. Rather, he kept focusing on his wife, his marriage, his love for his wife, and his original ambivalence about getting married. This was the subject matter that interested him. It was where his tension was focused, and so his wife was a very good candidate for the *who* with whom he was basically angry, though unaware of it. His love for her was believable, but what he apparently didn't understand was that it was possible to love and be angry with the same person, and that moreover, an emotional coexistence of that kind is all right, even normal. Apparently, he felt that to be angry with the person you love is equivalent to some kind of sin, and being aware of it, conscious of it, might therefore make him out to be a bad person.

It seemed that his wife was the identified *who*, and his repressed anger was about her. Furthermore, to understand his wish was also uncomplicated. His wish, five years ago when he married, was not to marry. Ambivalence is a tricky state. It seems to mean that you may want to do something and then again, you may not want to do that thing. Yet, ambivalence is never democratic; each side of the ambivalence does not get an equal emotional vote. The fact is that in ambivalence, the "no" vote is dominant. When the "yes" vote brings to bear pressures from other sources that subdue the "no" vote, then the person will indeed be able to engage in the action about which the ambivalence was originally concerned. In this patient's case, when his "no" was subdued or outvoted, he did indeed engage in the action about which the ambivalence was originally concerned. He married. His wish was not to marry. Yet, he did marry, but he seemed also to have married his ambivalence.

In this patient's case, his marriage, one might say, was based against his stronger ambivalent "no" vote, and in favor of his weaker, ambivalent "yes" vote. He had been suffering the consequences of that "yes" vote up to the present time with the symptom of selective agoraphobia. He was not phobic about just any open space; the symptom only appeared with respect to crossing bridges.

Understanding the Symptom

His wish had been not to marry yet. His wife became the *who* toward whom he was angry because of her power to sway him against his wish. Thus, going against his will, or his wish, disempowered him and then this disempowerment generated the anger that he repressed. He would have then correspondingly, developed this agoraphobic symptom based upon the definition that the symptom is the thwarted wish, fully realized. In some way, the agoraphobia would have had to be a symbolic reintroduction of his original ambivalence regarding his marriage.

Now, how does being panicked, and in the throes of an anxiety attack that generates the full flower of a compartmentalized phobia, satisfy one's basic wish not to marry yet? The possible answer to that question invites a psychoanalytic perspective of the symptom within the context of the symptom-code.

First of all, the symptom-code cannot answer each question directly. At times the code can lead to the bridge, but to get across, sometimes one needs a touch of the Socratic method. In this sense, the question becomes: What does a bridge do; that is, what purpose does it serve?

It may be that to understand the answer to that question is also to understand the meaning of the symptom. Of course, such meanings are educated guesses–hypothetical. The concern here is in the search for the truth of the interpretation–for its validity. With the reasonable certainty of the interpretation, it becomes more possible to make the unconscious conflict, conscious. Then, the mystery of the symptom that so defeats the patient with its otherworldliness and irrational existence, can be seen to be quite prosaic. In fact, it is probably the case, that no matter how bizarre a symptom seems, when it is unraveled, it is usually then seen as being basically simple. It becomes no longer something mysterious or to be feared, and certainly no longer other worldly or irrational. When it is unraveled, the symptom loses its power, and so its reason for being will usually cease to exist. So too, it was expected that with this patient, the bridge phobia would, for all intents and purposes, vanish.

So what does a bridge do? A bridge usually connects two bodies of land mass that without the bridge, would in an anthropomorphic sense, find it difficult, even impossible to be connected, that is, to relate-and in a real sense, without the bridge, these two land masses remain distinct and unconnected.

It could be that this kind of metaphor reflects the patient's unconscious conflict regarding the genesis of his relationship with his wife, from the beginning of his courtship, to his initial ambivalence about marrying, to his marriage, and to an ostensible repressed anger regarding what he may have considered to be, and may still consider to be, doing something against his wish. The wish, of course, in one sense, was to rid himself of his ambivalence, which he apparently could not do. Thus, it could be assumed that he had carried this conflict with him to the present, in the same configuration as it was in its initial state. Even though five years had elapsed since his marriage, nevertheless, in his psyche it is quite likely that the conflict with its derivative product of ambivalence about marriage, remained the same, intact, with time having no effect on it. The phenomenon of transference is a supportive underpinning to this notion of the possible stasis of psychic conflict, or of the resistance of psychic conflict to conditions of the real world. Of course, particular transferences can last a lifetime without any changes to their nature whatsoever, no matter what kinds of experiences the person has.

Thus, it may be that his bridge difficulty was really a difficulty in an unresolved conflict regarding his stated ambivalence that reflected isomorphically what he originally felt about marriage, five years earlier; that is, a tension about the bridge to marriage, and a corresponding tension about bridges that connect one land mass to another. Of course, assuming that these constituents of the symptom-code did, in fact, faithfully represent what was transpiring in his psyche, then: (1) knowing that his wife was the *who*; and (2) knowing that he was angry at her despite the fact that he also loved her; and (3) knowing that his phobic reaction to bridges really was a psychological equivalent to his five-year-old ambivalence; and (4) therefore, that the phobia itself, notwithstanding its selected and compartmentalized nature, was an ingenious realization of the part of the ambivalence that comprised his basic will–namely, not to marry against his wish; then, (5) it would be expected that the symptom itself would be seriously challenged, and perhaps dealt a death blow.

At such a point, in the symptom treatment, a *doing* thing would be important to implement. In this man's case the *doing* thing was seen to be some attempt on his part to surface a discussion with his wife about the entire issue of his ambivalence, and simultaneously to be sure to assure her that this ambivalence had nothing to do with his love for her. He would need to emphasize that the ambivalence was about *his* problem, *his* psyche, *his* history, *his* transference's, *his* early family life, and whatever else it suggested about *his* capacity to be ready for a departure from *his* nuclear family–before he and his wife ever even knew one another. Such a *doing* activity would surely nullify his behind *The Line* withdrawal with respect to the dynamics of the symptom concealed within his withdrawal – a withdrawal, so to speak, that because of its non-clinical nature, is hidden in plain sight.

In addition, the fact that his wish was negative, that it was an avoidant or indirect wish–that is, not to marry as a response to the powerful negative vector of his ambivalence–necessarily meant that it could be predicted that the symptom itself, rather than producing relief of tension, would instead, sustain or increase his tension; and that is precisely what had happened. His anxiety and panic regarding bridges apparently congealed into a selective agoraphobic reaction which only became ignited when he himself drove the vehicle. When others drove, none of this symbolism was evoked because as a passenger, his role as a decision maker was nullified.

Now the phrase "panic on the bridge" was revealed not to be about the steel, or girders, or span of the bridge at all. What it was really about was the steel and girders and span of the emotional bridge from the patient to his wife that, in addition, spanned five years.

Chapter 12
"I Can Hardly Move":
A Case of a Three-Day Migraine

The patient moved very slowly as he walked into the conference room of an out-patient clinic. He was wearing sun glasses and said that the light bothered him. However, it was clear that even with his dark glasses, he was squinting, and his face was pinched with pain. He was a 60-year-old man who was experiencing a three day migraine.

The room was filled with a dozen or so psychologists, social workers, and psychiatrists. The report that was read to those assembled stated that the patient was reassured by his physician that there was no physical basis for the migraine, and that the pain was certainly emotionally based; a severe tension headache caused by some psychological-emotional conflict.

This was not terribly reassuring to this man who had been suffering with the migraine for the previous three days, without any relief. It was so bad that he pleaded with his physician to get him some general anesthesia. He said, "I have to speak softly. I can't move too suddenly. It's like a vice in my head." He also indicated that this same kind of head pain had occurred on two other occasions in his life.

The report had also indicated that he was married with no children, and that he was born partially deaf. As it turned out, the fact was that he was born almost completely deaf, and this accounted for his awkward sounding speech. The crisis of his life, at the time of this conference, was that he and his wife were in financial straits. Apparently, he, along with many others, had been excessed from his job during an ongoing recession.

Since the migraine had appeared only three days earlier, it seemed unlikely that the direct pivotal stimulus for it concerned his job loss, which had happened more than two months earlier. However, because of his job loss, this couple had incurred a sizable amount of credit card and other debt, and it was then that the patient began to feel depressed. "We had to change our lifestyle immediately," he said. "I only feel depressed about this situation. Otherwise, I'm not depressed," he added.

The Initial Consultation

The initial consultation was followed by a smaller meeting because the patient was bothered by the larger meeting. In the first consultation the patient had told the assembled staff that because of their financial condition, his wife and he would now need to live with his wife's affluent sister, who lived in the Deep South. The plan was that the sister would take care of all financial matters. However, the patient was adamant about not wanting to go. "Even though we'll get a subsidy, and won't be paying any rent, and she'll pay all of our bills until I can find a job, I still don't like it," he said. He paused for a moment, and in an expostulation of anguish and protest, he further said, "I hate it, and I told her so."

Upon further investigation, the patient revealed that he was a member of one of New York City's oldest private clubs. He was particularly proud of the fact that to gain membership in the club was quite difficult, requiring recommendations as well as some evidence of distinguished work in a given professional field. Thus, the membership of the club consisted mostly of persons of letters, professors, politicians, entrepreneurs, and so forth. The patient gained entrance because he'd been active in community affairs, and had been on the Mayor's volunteer committee to tidy up the parks of the city. He had been the one to organize the fund raising for shovels, pick-sticks, rakes, and various other such items. The club, he said, was very important to him. Apparently, membership in the club elevated his sense of self-esteem, and, in addition, gave him an overall sense of achievement, and, he added, "even emotional security." It would be all for naught, he claimed. He was leaving.

The patient's objection to leaving led to an intense argument with his wife, who kept repeating to him the need to leave, with which paradoxically, he agreed. He knew it was the logical thing to do So, on the one hand, despite the fact that he knew the move was the only way to salvage themselves, on the other, he was still adamant about not wanting to go.

He was also quite clear about his hearing challenged condition, his hearing disability. He indicated that in the club, and for the first time in his life, no one cared about the way he spoke. Apparently, when he was a child, other children would occasionally imitate his somewhat awkward sounding speech. "It imprinted itself on my soul," he said. "But at the club no one cares about how I sound–they're only interested in how I think. And when it comes to thinking, I'm fine."

Many questions were being raised by members of the staff, and the session was becoming somewhat of a free-for-all. The patient complained of too much noise, and it was then that it was decided to meet in a smaller conference room with only three of the staff. The larger meeting adjourned, and the patient was escorted to the smaller room. It was in here that he further admitted to feeling horrible about his impending move, and repeated that he forgets about his arguments with his wife and starts thinking about how to actually manage and adjust to his new situation. In fact, his wife and he had already made arrangements for the transfer of furniture and various other of their possessions, and despite his protest, nevertheless he was immersed in the reality—the considerable planning regarding their relocation.

When pressed about the arguments, he recalled that he wanted to shout at his wife, "I can't go," but instead, he "beat around the bush." Then he indicated he would forget the arguments because he was too busy with the details of moving.

Applying the Symptom-Code

At the smaller meeting, he was asked whether, even at the present moment, at this meeting, did he feel angry at his wife? He denied this, but then remembered that several days earlier he and his wife were talking and in the midst of their conversation he had the fantasy not only of shouting at her, but rather screaming: "I can't move, I can't." He didn't do it. Rather, he again said, "I just beat around the bush."

In applying the symptom-code, it was a good bet that his wife was the *who*, and that not only was he angry at her, but more than likely, he was furious at her. The fact was that again, even though he knew he was angry at her, it was only a superficial knowledge. He was not at all aware of the extent of his anger, nor of its pervasive nature. His conscious thought about his anger was only that he was feeling conditionally angry at her; that is, only when they had their arguments. It was as if he felt that his anger had parameters; the anger started at the beginning of the argument, and ended when the argument was over. Thus, even though he believed his anger was time-limited, and even though he also consciously knew about some of it, what he didn't know was that much of this anger was in a repressed state, and that without any doubt, it was smoldering.

His wish was also easy to understand. Most prevalent was his *wish* not to move, not to relocate, not to relinquish his club membership. If the wish were to be satisfied, then he could retain his reassured self-esteem, essentially fueled by his membership in the club. And even though his wife was entirely unmalicious in her zeal for them to seek refuge with her sister, nevertheless the frustration of his wish was attributed to her. With respect to the content of his unconscious, so far as he was concerned, his wife was responsible for his many "d's"—*deflation, depression, despair,* and *demoralization,* as well as responsible for his many "dis's"—*disgust, dispiritedness, disorientation,* and *dislocation.*

The task here was to help him see that his anger was actually more pervasive than he thought, and quite likely, that this anger was attacking him and was the emotional culprit in the appearance of his migraine. When this interpretation regarding the connection between his anger and his migraine was surfaced, he tried to avoid its implication, but he would keep coming back to the point by saying: "So you think I'm really always angry at my wife underneath it all, and that's why I'm suffering with the migraine?" The idea definitely arrested his attention, and he couldn't quite leave it alone.

Understanding the Symptom

The special club he belonged to elevated his self-esteem. It was a compensatory agent for him. The question became: Compensating for what? The answer it seemed was that his membership in the club enabled him to feel whole, adequate, and not concerned with being deaf or speech challenged. This was the essence of the meaning of the symptom. The club meant adequacy. In his new living conditions with his wife's sister, he would be stripped of such compensatory currency, and therefore perhaps at that point he would need to confront what he considered his true reality–the misery of being inadequate, deaf, and sounding awkward when he spoke.

Thus, the salient issue was joined. He must have felt that to have the killer migraine was actually preferable to confronting this crucial issue of his life–his deafness, his awkward speech, and his sense of profound unwholeness. It may have been that with this new looming geographic relocation, he began to feel a descent into oblivion, that all the taunts he had experienced as a child were justified and now even validated. Thus, it was better to writhe in pain for three days rather than for him to confront the confounding problem of his life. Feeling the killer migraine served to distract him from the consciousness of his deafness, his awkward speech, and what he began to again feel – his other than normal self. No club, no normal self–only awkward speech and problems of the hearing challenged.

The upshot of this dynamic was that the presence of the migraine meant he was still adequate. That is, so long as he was distracted from the symbol of his inadequacy, his hearing and speech, then he remained adequate–albeit with a severe migraine. The migraine was therefore a displacement away from his deafness–a gratification of his wish to be adequate. Since, in the psyche, no wish will be denied, then by having the migraine, he got his wish–he remained adequate, and in addition his indirect wish not to move, produced a painful symptom.

In the smaller meeting, when all of this surfaced, he suddenly began talking without the severely pinched expression which had originally characterized his demeanor. He then also suddenly removed his sun glasses, and exclaimed: "The migraine is better. It's not a migraine. It's better." He exclaimed that it felt like geologic plates shifting; that is, he explained that in his head, he could feel as though different planes were shifting.

His migraine was actually cured on the spot. This occurred by the sheer power of surfacing the elements of the symptom-code and talking about them. He even looked younger. It seemed that the curative process was quite easily achieved here primarily because his anger toward his wife, the who, had not been at all heavily repressed. Rather, he was conscious of his anger toward his wife but had felt it was only related to his arguments with her. What he wasn't aware of was the full extent of his anger. It was at the point when he could see that his anger was all encompassing and was entirely and continuously directed at his wife, that he began to feel better. Then when it was interpreted to him that the migraine was pretty much preferable to confronting the whole issue of his hearing and speech, which he felt he was being forced to do by relocating and leaving the club, he became silent, and seemingly thoughtful, and it was then that he exclaimed he was feeling better.

In addition, it was suggested that he look into other clubs in his anticipated new environment, and that also with the locating of a professional position, he could create another productive venue, that in the end would serve him well.

Chapter 13
Doubled Over: A Case of Displaced Phallic Obsession

This case was unusual in several ways. First, the patient had been seeing a female therapist at an outpatient clinic, and only a chance encounter with him in the corridor leading to the therapy rooms led to his fervent request for a change to a male therapist. Second, he did not request this change of therapist because he was angry or in any other way opposed to his therapist. Rather he wanted to switch because he felt he couldn't say things that he needed to say, "In front of a woman–a nice woman like that."

When I first saw this man he was kind of in a doubled-over position, arms holding his stomach, standing somewhat bent over in the corridor leading to the therapy rooms. I asked him if he needed help and he squeezed out a "No," as though his stomach was in knots. He asked me if I was a therapist, said that his therapist was late, adding, "She's never late," and finally then said, "I think I need a male therapist."

He claimed he had things to say, "something that's not easy to talk about with a woman." After ascertaining that I was indeed a therapist, he asked me, on the spur of the moment, and without much apparent consideration, whether I would be his therapist. I suggested he talk it over with his therapist and then see how he felt. Before I had the chance to explain it further, he started: "I get doubled over all the time. It's about beautiful women, you know–built. When I see one in the street or anywhere, I feel like someone shot me in the stomach. It's so fierce that it doubles me over."

I told him again that I couldn't get involved, and that really, he should try to talk to his therapist about it. He disregarded me and whispered: "It's tits. They get me right in the labonza. Know what I mean? I just double over. It's like getting shot with a shotgun or something. And it hurts. I've gotta tighten my stomach muscles to get over it. What the hell is it?" He then pleaded with me to speak to his therapist, which reluctantly, I agreed to do. He said, "Okay, but don't say 'tits' to her. Say I said 'breasts.' But between you and me, breasts isn't it. It's tits! That does it to me."

At this point he was no longer doubled over. He had straightened up. He continued: "And you know that blonde secretary with the big ones down the hall? Well she just walked past me right before you showed up. And you saw–I was all messed up. I had to wait a while before I could straighten up. What's causing it? I can't imagine what's causing it."

What he was saying was also reminiscent of what a patient I had treated some years earlier had told me. That patient felt as though someone had just punched him in the stomach whenever he saw a woman in a tight sweater who had large breasts. That patient said it only happened when the woman was wearing a sweater, and he associated the feeling of being punched in the stomach with anxiety. Of course, the anxiety was his conscious experience that was, in all probability, radiating up from repressed anger.

"Doubled-over" interrupted my reverie by finally saying: "Listen, when you speak to her, tell her I like her, but I need to see a male therapist. I mean between you and me, I can't say shit to her. I mean I can't use words. I can't say fuck, or anything. Know what I mean?"

He told me who his therapist was, and I did, in fact speak to her. She agreed that it was very difficult for him to relate to her, and said that he was quite formal in the sessions and tried always to say the right thing. She thought that he would be spending too much time trying to talk to her in a relaxed fashion, if he would ever be able to at all. She mentioned that his attempt to use vocabulary that was socially acceptable was actually endearing, but despite her efforts to reassure him that it was all right to use the vernacular, he couldn't do it. I became "Doubled-Over's" therapist.

He was a 37-year-old man who was friendly and very talkative. He had never married, and as he put it: "I was the 'Last of the Mohicans' of my friends." Apparently, he was the only one of all of his friends who had not married and he felt that most of his problems about women, and doubling over, were probably somehow related to his loneliness.

The Initial Consultation

"Yes man, I, am, lonely!" He emphasized each word separately, it seemed, to reflect the emotional impact that he experienced about being lonely. "I even talk to myself in the street, and sometimes I don't realize that other people can hear me until it's too late. I know what that's about. I'm lonely. No one to talk to."

He regaled me with his history of ruminating on large breasts and indicated that he started having these feelings sometime in his 20's. He claimed to always have been moved or aroused by any girl or woman with an ample bust-line. He stated that it was more with women in clothes than it was when they were naked. "Naked tits," he said, "don't get me wrong, I like them, but it's better when she's in clothes. Like when I see the outline, and I can see that they're packed in and together, and that they're a little heavy, you know, like they weigh something." He went on to explain that the breasts not only need to be large – they have to protrude. He also said it was better when the woman was larger in stature rather than slight or short. But he also explained that "better" meant also worse because when it was at its best—when the woman was large in stature with large protruding breasts—it was then that his doubled-over reaction, like being shot in the stomach with a shotgun, would be the worst. So, he said, "best means worst, and worst means best. How do you cure that?"

This man was one of three siblings. His brother and sister lived on the West Coast and were only occasionally in touch with him. As he said, his friends were all married or away, and he stated that his main task each week was to figure out how to spend the weekend. He disliked going places alone because he felt a bit shy, and he was not good at unearthing social or other kinds of events that he might want to attend. Thus, each weekend became a drudge, and more often than not, he would simply while away the time.

Monday mornings became his favorite time of the week because it meant he could go to work, and the structure and requirements of his job would save him from boredom. It was at his job that he interacted with colleagues, thereby satisfying a portion of his need to be social. He worked in the financial affairs department of a large corporation and specialized in one facet of financial planning. He stated that he was also formal at work, as he was with his female therapist. It was only with his friends that he could let his hair down and relax.

To him, the main cue for feeling that he could be relaxed, was being in the presence of people with whom he could use profanity, colloquialisms, and all varieties of sexual allusions. His early history growing up on the West Coast was one within a lower socioeconomic context, and where his language was always peppered with profanity (or perhaps more accurately, where his profanity was always peppered with language).

"I tried thinking about the whole thing with psychology," he said. "The best I could come up with is that my loneliness is eating away at me, and that I really do want to get married, so that when I see a beautiful woman the way I described, I just feel it strongly in my stomach."

In further describing his preoccupations, he confessed to ruminating about the size of his penis which he referred to as his "dick." He said it was amazing that sometimes when looking at his penis in his bathroom mirror, it looked rather large, and that that made him feel good, while at other times, it looked small, and that he didn't like. He wondered whether his mood had something to do with such estimates, but reflected on the absurdity of it all; that is, how is a person's penis, measured in the flaccid state, or for that matter in any state, as both large and small, or for that matter, both adequate and inadequate, or moreover, either large enough or not large enough?

After he revealed his concern about his penis size, he also readily admitted to not being able to discuss this with his female therapist. His interest in this subject matter, and the amount of time he spent in this initial consultation talking about it, suggested that he had gotten to the crux of his symptom, and that a great deal of the therapy work, would have to be done, as it were, in his crotch.

He also described a recent scene in which he got drunk while at a dance because as he put it: "I saw this great looking chick with big ones, and I just couldn't go over to her. I was stuck. No nerve. So I got drunk instead." He indicated that the next day when he was sober and contemplated his previous evening's failure of courage, it was then that he realized just how worried he really was.

Applying the Symptom-Code

It was virtually impossible to identify any specific *who* with whom this patient was angry. There was no one person. Hence, almost by default, it became clear that what was happening to him was that he was becoming angry at each and every woman that affected him with his "shotgun in the stomach feeling." For one, that type of woman evoked an intense response in him, and second, despite his urgent need to possess such a woman, he was at best, shy and at worst unable to approach such a woman because of deeper psychological issues. Such a presumed deeper issue concerned strong inferiority feelings that subjectively confirmed for him his expectation that the woman would not respond to him positively; he felt she would not be attracted to him.

Thus, apparently his *wish* was to possess such a woman. Yet, with respect to his emotional life, the form in which the wish actually expressed itself was framed in the context of his prediction that the woman's most likely response would be an unrequited one. In essence, it boiled down to his wanting her, but his feeling that she would not want him.

His certainty that the woman, and not he, was the desired object, valued and hoped for, made it virtually impossible for him to navigate the treacherous contours of his dilemma. He could never feel equal to her. In contrast, he could only feel the presence of his need, along with the dreadful anticipation that this need would go unfulfilled. In view of this, it could be assumed that he was instantly angry at each of these women because he anticipated not only that they would reject him, but in his mind, that they had already rejected him even before any one of them ever laid eyes on him. He was so certain of this rejection, that the future tense was not a reality to him. The future tense morphed instantly into a past tense. It wasn't that she might not be attracted to him, it was that the verdict had already been made even before anything happened. He was convinced that whoever the woman was, she absolutely would not be interested in him even before anything happened.

Of course, since he would have felt instantly disempowered by this pre-rejection, it also can be assumed that the moment he spotted one of these women, he also became instantly angry, and correspondingly, instantly repressed the anger. Thus, he would never know he was angry. The only thing he knew was the overpowering feeling of how his stomach felt.

His *wish* therefore, as it expressed itself, was an avoidant, indirect one. He really wished that he not be rejected. This indirect form of the wish was derived from his sense of inferiority or inadequacy so that the symptom itself, ending with his doubled-over position, rather than alleviating discomfort, sustained and even intensified it.

In a nutshell, and with respect to the symptom-code: (1) his wish was not to be rejected; (2) the *who* was each large busted woman that evoked his shotgun-stomach reaction; and, (3) his anger at her for what he felt was an axiomatic rejection was instantly repressed.

Hence, his symptom of doubling over could be understood as the wish gratified. This meant that doubling over whenever he spotted a large busted woman in some way gratified his wish not to be rejected; that doubling over in pain meant that he actually could possess the woman. The question is, why did doubling over mean that? What did it mean that he needed to possess such a woman, but because he felt he couldn't, then he doubled over–wish gratified?

Understanding the Symptom

His two major themes in the session, as well as in subsequent sessions concerned first, his symptom of doubling over and its relation to seeing women with large protruding breasts, and second, a consistent focus on his penis size.

With respect to his focus on his penis, he easily revealed that from early on in his life, he would have fantasies of possessing a large penis and that at first, when he was an adolescent, in his fantasy he would exhibit it to girls and they would admire it, and later when he was older, the same fantasy would be applied to women, who also would admire it. Apparently, these fantasies were satisfying to him, and even to the present, as stated, he would feel relieved when he perceived his penis to be large.

Of course, his psychological understanding would ultimately need to include a growing awareness of and perhaps a sense of the synthesis of three issues: (1) How was his wish for companionship gratified by talking to himself? (2) How was his wish to possess the woman with large breasts realized by his shotgun-stomach and his doubling over? and (3) What was the meaning of his shifting perception with regard to the size of his penis?

Of course, prevailing wisdom has it that breasts represent the nurturing wish. Yet, in this case, his focus on breasts was not about his mother or the mother's breast, or mother's milk, or mother's presumed or even ostensible abandonment of him. It seemed that the connection of the issues concerned the equation of breast and penis. If he possessed the woman with large breasts, then he became adequate because presumably, the large breast represented the large penis. In such a case, whenever he created this equation, albeit unconsciously, he then would feel adequate. Thus, under such a condition of possessing the woman with large breasts, he would perceive his penis as large. This successful synthesis would work for him whenever he fantasized that the woman with large breasts was attracted to him. This would produce a feeling of pride in the size of her breasts. Of course, he never realized that he was only equating breast with penis, thus creating a scenario in which he could essentially feel proud of the size of his penis.

This was a phallic obsession in which the defense mechanism of displacement supported his repression, so that his focus was on her breast and not his penis. The reality was that his steady-state, his normal state, was one in which he considered his penis wanting in size. It was only when he fantasized the successful possession of the woman with large breasts that he was able to feel good about his size–to feel adequate. In his case, he felt successful only in the fantasy, and because of the repressed nature of the dynamic, he was never able to understand his unconscious primary connection of breast and penis. When, on the other hand he actually met a woman or saw a woman with large breasts, and because of the reality of the situation, could not fantasize, then he would instantly experience his shotgun-stomach symptom because he felt correspondingly instantly rejected by her, even though she was in no way a party to this emotional and psychological drama.

Another way of framing the conflict is to imagine that only in fantasy does he successfully achieve his wish not be inadequate, that is to say, only in fantasy is he able to achieve his wish to be adequate. In reality, his private noninteraction with a woman he randomly encounters, produces a thwarting of his wish, so that in his disempowerment, he becomes angry and represses the anger.

He becomes angry at the disempowerment because of not achieving the prize. To him the prize seems to be to possess the woman with the large breasts. However, the real prize for him is to feel he has a large penis. And when he is feeling rejected by the woman with large breasts, he then cannot have the large penis and ends up feeling his shotgun-stomach because when he can't have her, he's not conscious that it's his penis that is implicated. For him, consciously, it's just that his stomach hurts–a classic case of displacement upwards–in this case, penis to stomach.

Thus, the therapeutic job here, contributing to the alleviation of the symptom, in addition to surfacing the unconscious "facts," would be to enable him to gain additional self-esteem and begin to value himself, and not displace these concerns onto his penis through a displacement onto large breasts.

It was the dominant force of self-doubt that needed here to be therapeutically tackled. This would ultimately constitute the *doing* component of the symptom-code ultimately escorting him out of behind *The Line* into an in front of The line position.

Part III
The Clinical Casebook: Inaccessible Symptoms

These are symptoms that are generally characterized by any combination of the following factors, as being:

1. deeply engraved psychotic, or psychotic-like, and that have usurped the entire personality;
2. chronically entrenched and/or somatized;
3. a function of an organic brain syndrome, genetic anomaly, or a particularly thin ego;
4. a function of a catastrophic anger or rage implosion based upon an experience of profound helplessness;
5. no longer an alien facet of the psyche but rather as having usurped the psyche.

With respect to the nature of the anger or rage implosion, such inaccessible symptoms are so designated because the repressed anger:

1. is of the severest *magnitude* so as to have threatened almost all, or literally, all aspects of the psyche;
2. is of such *intensity* that the psyche anticipates its imminent demise;
3. is of such sufficient *depth* that the psyche may anticipate a foreboding of being imminently cleaved;
4. is so *chronic* that the psyche is likely to have already succumbed to the symptom.

Chapter 14
The Psychology of Blushing: Involuntary Disclosure of Success Wishes

In Part II of this volume, symptoms were presented that could be treated by psychotherapy because they were not chronically entrenched. Nor, for the most part, did they reflect a severe pathology. Further, such symptoms were not chronically somatized or reflective of some organic condition or genetic anomaly; that is, they were of relatively recent onset. Rather than having engulfed the personality, the symptoms remained as only a facet of the personality, one that was retained in the personality, characteristically as an alien presence.

Thus, such symptoms could be directly approached via the symptom-code, in which the *wish*, the *anger*, and the *who*, could often be identified. The symptom then could be further isolated within the personality, and finally penetrated, unraveled, and erased. This could be accomplished because the patient's resistance to understanding the symptom could be analyzed. Repression, therefore, could be more directly dealt with, leading to a greater probability of the dissolution of the symptom through the undermining of resistance to change, and the subsequent lifting of the repression.

In Part III, symptoms will be presented that resist psychotherapy treatment, and therefore render the power of the symptom-code rather ineffective with respect to cure, especially immediate cure. Thus, the inherent differences in treatment between symptoms accessible to the symptom-code can be clearly distinguished from those symptoms that are inaccessible and that resist the talking cure.

Blushing, is as an example of a symptom that resists cure; that is, a chronic symptom that has been a characteristic psychological feature of the person's entire life. This kind of symptom can really only be challenged, but not usually undermined, by the simple use of the symptom-code. This sort of symptom and its embeddedness in the subject's psychological context will need far more therapeutic work for it to be subdued. Even with such additional therapeutic work, curing such symptoms is frequently an unsuccessful hit or miss situation.

The explanation for this kind of resistance to cure, concerns the difference in what it is that constitutes a *symptom*, and what it is that defines a *trait*. There are symptoms which, because of their longevity, as well as how they have been knitted into the fabric of personality, that become in psychoanalytic parlance, ego syntonic. This means that the complement of personality traits that together comprise one's personality profile, can contain certain characteristic symptoms that become traitlike. For example, since all people are consistent in their behavior, then even those who are unstable, unpredictable, or unglued, can be characterized by their typical personality traits. "She is shy and will blush easily," is a comment that reflects a person's typical behavior or attitude, and, when described this way, the behavior is recognized by anyone who has known the person. "Yes, she is shy," would be the acknowledgment, "and further, we all know that she always blushes when she is in (such and such) a situation." Or, the symptom that is trait-like begins to entirely characterize the person as a shorthand: "Oh, you mean blushing Sally?"

In other words, there are symptoms that become characteristic of the person and are so entrenched and chronic within the amalgam of the person's cluster of traits, that for all intents and purposes, it is no longer meaningful to distinguish that symptom from any of the person's other traits.

From a psychological point of view, however, this homogenization of a symptom into the class of phenomena identified as personality traits, is only descriptive. From the clinical-scientific point of view, indeed, even though the symptom is now also functioning as a trait, nevertheless, that symptom also remains a different species from that of traits. In this respect, the symptom of blushing, for example, when characteristic of a person's typical reaction to stimuli, conditions, or circumstances, is truly a trait but also truly a symptom.

The difference between the trait of *shyness* and that of *blushing* concerns the ability to voluntarily control the state. Usually, traits at least temporarily, can be voluntarily controlled. The person cannot voluntarily and permanently eliminate a so-called natural shyness, even though under certain more familiar circumstances, shyness can be less evident, or can be better controlled, or even that the person is not at all shy under certain conditions of familiarity.

In contrast and with respect to blushing, the same phenomenological variation is absent. The person always blushes in response to certain stimuli. Thus, there is a psychology to the symptom of blushing, which in the original onset of the symptom, is different from the psychology of the personality trait; namely, that the blushing initially sits apart from traits. Yet, a blushing symptom can become part of the person's trait structure. When it does, it will retain its immunity to conscious decision making. Thus, the symptom is not subject to voluntary control, and like all symptoms (and unlike all traits), and despite its presence in the domain of traits, the symptom is both similar and different from a trait. In this sense, the blushing symptom, like any symptom that insinuates itself into the domain of traits, takes on the complexion of a trait–becoming part of the personality profile–while also retaining its configuration, as a symptom.

The Symptom-Code and the Infrastructure of Blushing

Despite resistance to the symptom-code with respect to the talking cure, blushing, as a symptom follows the same rules in its construction and formation as does any symptom. Presumably, there was an original thwarted wish, and a consequent sense of personal disempowerment regarding this unfulfilled wish. This experience is followed by a reflexive angry feeling toward a particular person, a *who*, the object of the angry feeling. If a sense of the impossibility of expressing the anger directly to that *who* follows, then the anger will be repressed. Ultimately, the wish emerges as the symptom, albeit in perverse or neurotic form.

In the case of the blushing symptom, its manifest or descriptive problem concerns how the person feels about it. Usually, the subject of the blushing reports feeling horrified at being noticed. The fear or apprehension of being noticed, and therefore "sticking out," bringing attention to the self (especially if that attention to the self is in any way aggrandizing), is the worst fear. It is in such a circumstance that blushing appears. Of course, there are those who blush, but not during conspicuous moments. These people seek attention, and yet under certain circumstances are plagued with blushing responses. Thus, although blushing usually concerns the issue of conspicuousness, there are other circumstances that can also call forth the blushing response.

With respect to the psychology of blushing therefore, usually, but not always, the person's worst fear is to be noticed. This issue of being noticed can take many forms. For example, winning an argument or calling attention to oneself in direct or even in inadvertent ways, qualify as pivotal stimuli to the blushing response.

The manifest level to the blushing phenomenon, therefore, consists of a dread, apprehension, or fear of standing out. Yet what happens is that the person's worst fear is realized. In contrast to not wanting to stand out, the person's face turns crimson, or darker, which paradoxically, makes the person really stand out. The person, the subject, can feel the blush, and further, feels existentially embarrassed, even horrified, thinking that others are also seeing it.

A Case of Blushing in a 70-Year-Old Businessman

"You saw me almost blushing, didn't you." That was what this patient asked me after he mentioned that he became quite wealthy when he finally sold his stock in the pharmaceutical company he founded. Even he, a 70-year-old man, needed to hurry, to rush past the moment when he felt himself blushing. He began talking about other facets of his business in order, with great effort, to blunt what he experienced as this personally embarrassing blushing characteristic. But he stopped in the middle of this new story to ask me the question about my noticing his "almost blushing."

Thus, he would not even acknowledge to himself that he blushed nor that it was evident to those who were looking at him. Apparently, he had convinced himself that he was able to morph the blushing moment into a segue that he felt averted the obvious and visible evidence of his blushing. Yet, his notion of an "almost blushing" incident was not at all valid. Despite his illusion that he could avoid blushing, it was plainly not true. In this man's case, the blushing was not crimson red. He was a dark complected man and his blushing appeared as a slightly darker skin tone.

He acknowledged having had this problem all of his life and feeling uncomfortable about it since he first began experiencing it in grammar school more than 60 years earlier. He had discussed it in two therapy experiences but reported no success whatever in overcoming it.

Applying the Symptom-Code

This man's symptom was integral in his personality, and not merely an aspect of it. As pointed out in the preface of this book, his symptom qualified as one of those that are unlikely to respond to the powers of the symptom-code. His was a symptom that had integrated itself into the amalgam of traits that composed his characteristic personality profile. As such, his blushing impulse had attached itself to the entire underlying circuitry of his personality, and was not encapsulated as a separate entity, outside of the main template of his personality.

Nevertheless, although curing him of his blushing would be a difficult task, it would still be possible to apply the symptom-code, in order to understand what the symptom meant. First, it was necessary to define his basic *wish*. Next, it needed to be understood that his presumed lifelong *repressed anger* had become knitted into his personality – habituated. Third, it needed to be assumed that there was an original *who*, who in his more than 60-year past, was associated with this repressed anger.

In questioning him, it became evident that in his childhood home, a pious home, *pride*, as a value, was strongly discouraged, even perhaps, prohibited. Thus, this man was always taught to minimize any personal achievement. Apparently, it was the ethos of the home that only modesty would be valued. Boasting especially was prohibited and even considered to be sinful. The wish for recognition, therefore, was necessarily relegated to his solipsistic unconscious–the only place it could reside. Thus, whenever something he said approached a discernible assertion of pleasure or pride in his aspirations, accomplishments, or achievements, involuntarily, he would blush.

The point is that his wish had been translated into the symptom, albeit it in a perverse form. In this person's case, this translated symptom also occurred because in order for a rather normal expression of pride to occupy some place in his overall repertoire of responses, ironically it surfaced as blushing. Of course the paradoxical, oxymoronic, and fascinating fact here is that in not wanting to *face* any feelings of pride that he may have harbored, his *face* showed that his underlying, unconscious, true feeling, was prideful.

The point here also implies that even with respect to unconscious forces, he could not express pride in anything he had accomplished. But because he couldn't have his wish, because the wish to express pride was thwarted, then according to the symptom-code, it is proposed that he became instantly angry. His anger thus would have been related to the prohibition against expressing himself normally, in this case, feeling consciously proud of his achievements. The thwarted wish, however, would give him the opposite sense, of weakness, helplessness, disempowerment. The anger would have been his way of momentarily empowering himself. Of course, the problem was that he could not, or would not show this anger, whether or not he was conscious of it, for fear of revealing his original, concealed pridefulness.

The anger, by definition, became repressed because he had a very definite symptom. It could be assumed therefore, that it was his father (whom he indicated was the disciplinarian and decorum-governor of the home, the one who set the rules about comportment), who was the *who* at whom, as a child, this man was angry.

The psychoanalytic implication is that he would need to be conscious of his unconscious anger toward his father, and to examine and work on it, to make it conscious, and then to do something that relates to the original prohibition against owning his personal achievements. It is proposed that until that happened the symptom would be sustained as part of his personality-trait system, and not as a separate part of his personality, specifically as a compartmentalized, alien symptom-characteristic.

In his present state of knowing, what happened was that whenever he reached a point in conversation with others in which his accomplishments and achievements appeared, especially in bold relief, then he became angry, because he couldn't show his pride, and then at once repressed the anger. His blushing appeared, which represented his true underlying wish to be noticed, a wish gratified, albeit in this translated, perverse form. This presumed original wish to be seen, was now therefore realized. Getting red in the face, gets you seen-ultimately, an involuntary disclosure of success--wish gratified.

A Case of Blushing in a 40-Year-Old Librarian

This woman was a cooperative person who, like the patient in the clinical illustration above, was also quite concerned with propriety, and was modest to a fault. She indicated that her career as a librarian was suitable for her. She was the youngest of five sisters and was happy to be one of them. She indicated that they were all quite supportive of one another and considered one another to be each other's closest ally.

The patient's two main personality problems were that first, she claimed to be, and was in fact, extremely deferent in her behavior toward others. She would be the one to always permit others the right-of-way, and generally she felt awkward about interactions in which her contribution was seen as effective, intelligent, or valuable. In clinical terms, it was difficult for her to assert her everyday normal entitlements without feeling, as she said, "too forward or too egotistical." Second, she would never assert any sort of pride in what she did, and in a profoundly minimizing stance, would feel better, as she stated, "losing rather than winning."

She also always felt uncomfortable whenever she was praised. Under such circumstances she would involuntarily blush a bright red. She was a fair skinned woman so that her blushing was red hot, and correspondingly, she always felt exceedingly embarrassed by it. She was never able to cure it, and had been suffering with this malady, this symptom, all of her life: "As long as I can remember," she said.

Applying the Symptom-Code

This woman was the sister in her sibling group who was most interested in maintaining harmonious family relationships. As the youngest in the family and "since early on," she said she had always felt secure as one of the five. She was grateful that her sisters accommodated her, and she was always the one to do sacrificial things for them.

In investigating her sibling relationships further, it became clear that she was always acutely aware of never besting her sisters, and hated any competitive games in which she participated. She always had a bad feeling about winning anything when it was one of her sisters at the losing end, and she claimed that often she would deliberately "not play well so as not to win." Whenever she won, she would automatically blush, and was petrified each time that occurred, knowing full well that the blushing was imminent and that there was nothing she could do to prevent it.

Thus, as in the previous case, this woman never permitted herself to express or demonstrate anything concerning pride. She felt that to express pride would mean that she was better than her sisters, and on her part, this was always a conscious, yet horrible thought.

Applying the symptom-code to this case revealed possible avenues leading to the meaning of her blushing symptom. First, her basic wish and the impossibility she felt of realizing it, is possibly an easy one to understand. It seemed that her protestations of doing anything in the world but win, revealed the opposite predilection—namely that she would desperately want to win, but by no means did she feel emotionally or psychologically equipped to do so. Apparently, her greatest fear was in possibly losing the affection and support of her sisters. The thwarted wish presumably created feelings of disempowerment as well as angry feelings, which she could never acknowledge. In this respect, the anger, because it could not be directly expressed to its intended *who* (a sister perhaps), necessarily needed to be repressed. The wish was then translated into the symptom of blushing. In her attempt to avoid being seen, by winning, for example, the symptom of blushing created the circumstance in which her basic wish was realized, albeit in perverse form-when she blushed, she was seen, and vividly so.

It was assumed, therefore, that her truest unconscious wish was to be the winner. And if by chance she won, or came close to winning, she always ended up blushing. The blushing also necessarily meant that she was angry at someone. In this case, the someone, the *who*, would have been one of her sisters or some other transferential sister-equivalent. In this sense, it could be hypothesized that her competitive strivings were adumbrated by any particular sister-figure against whom she needed to be less than successful.

It could easily be further hypothesized that this woman's blushing reflected an involuntary disclosure of success wishes. It could be assumed that she always wanted to be proud of her talents and accomplishments, and wanted to display her successes, to take pride in them, feel joyous about them. Yet, her belief may have been that should she express her success, unencumbered with apprehension, then some dire happening could result and her relationship with the *who* could possibly be forever contaminated. It further seemed that the prohibition against ever feeling proud of herself, or especially of expressing such pride, was what her blushing symptom was really all about. She had no sense of entitlement because to assert her needs as a first among equals would have been tantamount to permanently damaging the relationship between her and her sister or sister-figure, the presumed *who*.

Thus, this woman needed to remain in the background, with no real entitlements, no ability to feel normal about competitive games of any kind, and no insight into how terrified she must have been at her own repressed anger or rage. It is quite likely that the anger about her massively repressed state was too much for her to manage. Her particular personality pattern was such that she would continually reject any more publicly visible position for a more inconspicuous one. Of course, whenever she said or did the slightest thing that seemed smart or valuable, in any way that was noticeable, she would instantly blush. It was the blushing, however, of someone with an unconscious impulse that involuntarily disclosed the presence of success wishes.

A Case of Blushing in a 28-Year-Old Physician

"It would always happen in class," he said. "All my life, wherever I was in school, even in medical school, it would happen. The damned blushing."

This was a man who, to begin with, had a fair complexion with rosy cheeks. He was physically conspicuous because of his girth and height. He was a large person, who, despite his blushing symptom, nevertheless was gregarious and actually sought the spotlight. In his case, the blushing would occur if in any discussion, he made a mistake about some fact, or if someone proved him wrong. It was under such conditions that he would feel wounded, and as a consequence, would blush. Other than being wrong or getting some facts jumbled, or doing something awkwardly, he would not blush. Instead, and with relish, he could win contests and be the center of attention. Thus, the blushing symptom in this man was quite different from the blushing symptom for each of the other previous case examples discussed, even though there exist thematic strands that tie together the blushing symptoms of all three cases.

This man was a cultivated, highly intelligent, well educated, and erudite person. He took much pride in his profession and was careful to comport himself as he understood it necessary for a physician to do. His intellectual style was aggressive and he had a wonderful and easy command of language. Along with this, he was merciless toward others who he felt were not equal to whatever the intellectual task was that they had assumed. In such cases he would confront the person in a way that could be embarrassing to that person. This, despite the fact that if the situation were reversed, and he was the one challenged, his embarrassment, especially if he knew he was wrong, would be great, and without a doubt would cause him to blush a bright red, from the base of his neck to the dome of his bald skull. Nevertheless, he showed no empathy to others and could force others into these embarrassing intellectual encounters.

Applying the Symptom-Code

In this man's case, the *wish* that was presumably thwarted could be defined as one, that in a strange way, recapitulated his growing-up experiences. The *who*, it seemed was his father, who would constantly test him on all sorts of information regarding a wide array of subject matter. As a child, his pleasure was in getting the answer right. The problem was that his father would increase the complexity of the questions so that each and every episode of these question and answer periods would end with this man not knowing something. Then he would feel that his wish to be accepted and loved by his father was interfered with in the face of the father's distinct disapproval, or even sarcasm, regarding either the son's wrong answer or inability to answer altogether. Thus, in effect, each of these episodes was designed by his father to begin with success and end in failure. The objective then, in this "game," was to get his son to fail, to be disappointed. This kind of torment had continued all through this man's formative years.

The suggestion that this sort of template underpinned all of his blushing experiences was reasonably supported by his observation that he always blushed when finally he didn't get the answer. "I always noticed it when I couldn't answer or when I got the wrong answer. Then I would blush."

In this particular case, there was little doubt that his father was the *who* toward whom he was angry. After the anger was repressed, his blushing then possibly became the perverse expression of his wish to be noticed, to be the winner, to be loved. And even to the present time, and despite his professional stature, his blushing seems to be an involuntary disclosure of success wishes.

The application of the symptom-code presented here, would, in all likelihood, not have the power to erase such a blushing symptom because of how this symptom, over many years, became organized in the personality; that is, because of the symptom's chronicity it had become embedded in this man's personality trait structure, and was no longer an encapsulated product of his psyche. On the level of trait then, the blushing symptom was no different from his aggressive trait of intellectually challenging others as his father had done to him. Yet, the key to his blushing concerned his strident yearning for success, as though he had never resolved the need for his father's complete, unconditional approval, and in a manner in which the end result of any interaction, would be a winning and not a losing strategy.

Commonalities of the Cases

In all three cases, the vectors of these respective wishes, was to avoid something. In all three cases, the indirect, avoided "something" (wish) reflected variations on the theme of the management of success and failure. Therefore, because these wishes were indirect, then the symptom itself was painful. And indeed, in all three cases, blushing itself was extremely embarrassing and more or less painful to each of the subjects.

Furthermore, because of the resistive, chronic nature of these blushing symptoms–as samples of personality trait structure, and no longer merely as solely encapsulated symptoms that exist apart from the domain of personality trait structure–these patients, it was predicted, would find it more difficult to cure the symptom by resolving the conundrum of symptom as trait. This conundrum consists of prying loose the symptom from the domain of traits, and transporting it to the region of the psyche reserved for products alien to the personality, in this case to the domain of wishes and symptoms. Then with respect to the blushing symptom itself, it is a symptom-condition in a behind *The Line* state needing much work in order for it to shift to a more in front of *The Line* position signifying its readiness to be successfully treated with the symptom-code.

Chapter 15
"No Writing!": A Case of Delusional Self-Incrimination

In this case, the particular inaccessible symptom that will be described was a highly visible, encapsulated one, embedded within an unusual delusional system. The symptom was so entrenched and so delusional that in examining the case, it became difficult not to be struck with the notion that what we were looking at was the anatomy of a psychosis. Yet, it was a psychosis without hallucinations, general distortions, word salads, tangential thinking, flat affect, incoherence, or any other conventional criterion used to diagnosis psychosis. The psychosis was, in derivative form, exclusively reflected in the delusion, which was a distortion, but highly specific, one that did not contaminate other aspects of the subject's cognitive organization. What it did do, however, was contaminate the subject's primary relationship–it contaminated his partner's ability to be with him, because to live with such a specific distortion in a partner, and to hear about it incessantly, would be too much for any normal, balanced person.

The patient was a man in his 50's who was a crackerjack salesperson in the men's department store of a well-known clothing shop. He was the single most productive salesperson despite a tremendous handicap in the administration of his job. All of his coworkers knew about his idiosyncrasy (what they called "crazy"), and unfortunately, all took advantage of it.

The symptom was one in which the patient could do everything required of him as a salesperson except commit anything to writing. "No writing," he would say. He could not bring himself to write, and therefore, would not write. He was naturally intelligent, even gifted, and despite only a high-school education, was an avid reader, was quite literate and in fact, wrote well. Yet, under no circumstance would he put anything in writing.

Now, of course, this was difficult for him because he needed to write sales slips. His solution was to get various other salespeople to do it for him. The catch was that these other salespeople charged him a percentage of the sale to write the slip. In street parlance this is known as, "paying the vig." Since he was extremely productive as a salesman, then the "vig" each week was considerable, so because of this problem approximately 15% of his income went to the other sales people. No matter what his wife said or how she implored him to write the slips himself, his consistent mantra was: "No writing!"

This case is an example of the distinction that needs to be made between a symptom that is entirely isolated in the personality versus one that infiltrates the personality so that rather than only being an aspect of the personality, the symptom *becomes* the personality. In this case, despite the fact that the symptom remained encapsulated, nevertheless, it also influenced his entire personality. Despite the fact that he could function in all other ways, nevertheless, his symptom was so pervasive within his work life, and so intrusive with respect to the space it occupied in his marriage, that the symptom itself began to characterize his personality. The symptom therefore, became his most visible, dominant trait-characteristic. People who worked with him would laugh at him as though his problem was all there was to him.

Since this symptom had been plaguing him for the past 30 years, then naturally he had not written sales slips for that 30-year period, so that the possibility that his symptom could easily be cured through psychotherapy and by the application of the symptom-code, was rather unlikely.

The question became one of attempting to identify his basic *wish*, identify his *repressed anger*, and identify the *who* with whom he was presumably angry. Because this was such a chronic, long-standing symptom, it was also evident that the original *who*, also had surrogates in this patient's everyday life. Thus, with respect to the talking cure, and because of the encapsulated psychotic nature of his delusional symptom, the problem here was clearly that of an inaccessible symptom. When the details of his reason for not writing such sales slips were uncovered, then the encapsulated psychosis, as portrayed vividly in his delusion, was revealed. He was now also depressed because his wife had left him, and medication along with psychotherapy was seen as the best course of treatment.

The Delusion

This patient's wish became understandable after he admitted that he would not write sales slips because he felt whatever he wrote would implicate him in some crime. He also admitted to feeling uncomfortable whenever he read in the daily newspaper or saw on television news of some terrible crime. His discomfort in reading or hearing such news was such that he felt vulnerable, and believed he would be apprehended by the police for the commission of the crime. Thus, it may be possibly conceived that his fear about writing anything concerned an imaginary impulse that he anticipated, that might jump out of him and incriminate him in whatever crime or wrongdoing was reported in the news.

The main problem for him was the distinction between what he knew and what he felt. What he knew is that he really didn't commit any crime at all. Yet, he was gripped by an obsessive, all consuming feeling that, in fact, he did do something wrong, and that this wrongness would be revealed should he write anything at all. Thus, for him, "knowing" had very little power, while "feeling" was compelling. It was a case of a "knowing" that was obsessively gnawing at him, and a "feeling" that was paranoid. In one person – the obsessive versus the paranoid – the paranoid was always victorious.

Thus, simply stated, he was basically afraid that if he wrote anything down in black and white, he would not be able to control his impulse to confess, so that what he wrote would turn out to be his confession. He was guilt ridden and this feeling permeated his very being.

In a deeper sense, with respect to his basic self-image and ego, at the core of his personality it certainly could be assumed that he felt himself to be completely imperfect, incomplete, inadequate, and inferior, and was most likely furious about this self-assumed inferiority. Thus, this delusional thinking regarding his self-incrimination was a direct reflection of a psychosis. The delusion was all-consuming and he continually acted it out.

Because the entire syndrome was so chronic and so pervasive, the thought of succeeding with this patient in a psychotherapeutic endeavor in the absence of medication would in all likelihood have been folly. It is an example of attempting to understand and treat an ambulatory character psychosis in only partial lifelong remission. The remission was partial because, he retained the delusional thought. Yet, in all other spheres of his life, he was in tact.

Applying the Symptom-Code

The patient supplied only an outline, a sketch of his history, but enough to begin to speculate, however tentatively, about the underpinnings of his symptomatology, despite the fact that his memories of childhood were sparse, and therefore, it was difficult to pin down specifics.

The patient was an only child and his parents were disciplinarians. He indicated that there was not much affection in the home and the memories that remained with him mostly concerned what he thought was his mother's inattentiveness and punitive style, and what he thought was his father's sarcasm. For example, he remembered that he felt he could never get what he wanted. He was not sure that was quite the case, but he said it always felt that way.

Whatever the truth, it seemed that his dominant feeling toward his parents was, in the most general sense, quite negative, and in the more specific sense, may have been and continued to be, a very angry one. This speculation was supported by his memory that he thought they were once almost killed by a truck in a traffic mishap. He was a young teenager at that time, and he had the thought that if they indeed were killed, he would be free and could do the things he wanted to do. But he wasn't sure about the memory. He seemed to also remember feeling guilty (and it can possibly be assumed, ashamed about such a thought), and confessed that, "To this day I still think about it and I think maybe if that's what I thought that then I wanted them dead. I try to put it out of my mind, but sometimes I can't."

He only had vague memories of his father, describing his father as a nonpresence. He also reported not even having a clear memory of his mother. The fragmentary, yet detailed reportage of his relationship with his father was of a "drinking man who never talked, and mostly did what my mother wanted." The patient could not recall a single instance in which his father gave him something he asked for or countermanded his mother's refusals.

The speculation that might be made from this rather sketchy history of his early life, concerns how the symptom-code might be applied to an understanding of his symptom structure. In this case, identifying the *who* was difficult. Was it his mother or father? He was only somewhat aware of the negative feelings toward each of them. However, even though he was vaguely aware of his dissatisfaction toward his parents, it is probably safe to assume that it was really anger or rage toward them that remained unconscious.

It is proposed that his *repressed anger* was directed toward a specific *who*, mother or father. Part of the problem was his inability to produce clear portraits of his parents, or for that matter, of any other possibly important figures of his formative years.

The *wish*, is probably not difficult to guess. Since it would seem that his guilt reveals some basic rage against each of his parents – a guess based mostly on his obsessive, intrusive memory of thinking it would have been good had they been killed by the truck – then the rage he presumably felt, and continued to feel into adulthood, can translate from a wish that it would have been good had they been killed by the truck, into his wish to kill one or the other himself. It seems likely that his thought that he wanted the truck to do it, may already have been a translation of his chronic rage toward them, so that the truck was really a substitute object representing his own primary wish.

This rage was likely the equivalent of a wish to kill. Usually people can have such wishes, but they are harmless and remain on the level of wish, fantasy, and even on the manifest level of figure of speech. In this patient's case, perhaps the original wish developed, as suggested above, as a chronic and intense one, and it may be that he didn't have the resilience to see it as different from behavior. In his behind *The Line* withdrawal and fantasizing, thinking became equivalent to doing. Thus, he felt guilty that he had committed a crime – one of the ultimate crimes. It can be speculated that the distorted dynamics of his psyche began to govern and even dominate his personality, and even though he knew he didn't do it, nevertheless, his feeling that he did do it may have prevailed and triumphed over what he actually knew. It could have been that in the organization and tyranny of his psyche, as stated, *knowing* had very little power, while *feeling* was compelling.

Thus, as a strategy, not writing made sense. It meant that because unconsciously he had convicted himself of murder, then not writing kept him both in a guilt-free state, and at the same time enabled him to avoid the legal procedure for the crime, and, in addition, to avoid incarceration or worse. He could also be guilt-free because in the acting-out of the symptom of not-writing, the meaning of the symptom could remain unconscious; that is, because he acts out the symptom, then he doesn't have to know that he killed either his mother or father, which unconsciously, he, of course, in all likelihood, believed he had done.

This definition of acting out as described earlier, is the classic psychoanalytic definition; that is, that acting out is an attempt to do something rather than know something. In this patient's case, the doing presumably was expressed by enacting the symptom, and the not-knowing concerned his imagined self incrimination in a parent's ostensible murder.

With respect to the symptom-code then, the hypotheses here include: that his *wish* was to be free; *repressed anger* was identified; and, the *who*, of course, was hypothesized to be one of his parents, presumably toward whom the original rage was directed. Finally, it should be remembered, as reported in Part I, of this book, that a direct wish produces a symptom that relieves tension, while an avoidant wish is defined as indirect, and produces a symptom that sustains or increases tension. In this patient's case, his wish was a direct positive one –to do something rather than avoid something. The "to do something" was the wish to be free. Symbolically, whenever his symptom of not writing was acted out, it meant he was free because the culprit parent was dead – murdered by him – and further, the memory of the murder therefore kept unconscious. Hence there was a relief of tension each time he didn't write.

Of course, this entrenched symptom, which at all costs and with respect to his delusion, apparently needed to be protected, reinforced, and fortified, kept him behind *The Line* in an insular obsessive/paranoid withdrawal – albeit encapsulated – and made it impossible for him to be front of *The Line*, in a reality position.

The postscript here is that his father died of throat cancer ten years earlier when the patient was in his mid-40's; his mother, still quite extant, and in her late-70's.

Chapter 16
"I'm not Going to Work Today":
A Case of Agoraphobia

"I'm not going to work today." That quote was the first crystallized conscious hint of the problem in a 60-year-old woman who for the past 20 years, had worked as a bookkeeper for the same firm. She had never married, and despite her modest income, owned her own luxurious condominium apartment in a large metropolitan area. In addition, she owned an expensive luxury automobile, and her closets were literally jammed with the latest and most expensive tailor-made clothing. She vacationed twice a year for a month at a time. She never cooked for herself, and dined in expensive restaurants. All of this considered, her only visible source of income was that from her job as bookkeeper.

Her problem began with her initial statement, "I'm not going to work today," that she made to herself, out loud, and ended with her repeating out loud: "As a matter of fact, I'm not going to work, period."

This is how she reported the revelation that she was feeling different. In this case of a woman with severe agoraphobia, it could be predicted, as in the previous chapter of a case of delusion, that psychotherapy treatment would not be the efficacious sole strategy of choice. In the previous chapter, the therapy alone would have been impossible because of the chronic, entrenched nature of the problem, and because the symptom was encapsulated as a psychotic delusion, and further because the patient's memory of past people and events was quite vague. This made it difficult to capture the memory of the specific *who* with whom he had been angry.

Similarly, with the present case, psychotherapy alone could not solve the problem or cure the symptom, because a severe, even cataclysmic implosion of rage was assumed to be the cause. Moreover, this implosion is assumed to have been so devastating, that the anger-debris was, most likely scattered throughout her psyche. It would be impossible, therefore, to collect the anger and reconstitute it into the original rage reaction; that is, to reconstitute the memory of the *who* as it is connected to the rage. An effective therapy without medication was thus precluded. And this conclusion seemed valid, even in the face of her very conscious identification of the *who*.

Along with a medication regimen, a psychotherapeutic process was undertaken with this woman in a quest to stem the tide of the accelerating agoraphobia. The point was that she was deteriorating, the agoraphobia was accelerating, and she was set on the worst possible pathological course. By the time the patient began treatment, she was unable to be away from her apartment. As fortune would have it, she was able to visit a therapist whose office was at a separate entrance to the building in which she lived. However, these visits required her to leave the building, walk four or five steps to this other door, and yet, even this was only possible for a while. Despite the medication and therapy sessions, after only some sessions, the agoraphobia became resistant to any sort of intervention.

In short order, not only would she not go to work, but she would not leave the lobby of her apartment building. Soon thereafter, she could not leave her apartment. Still later, she had decided she would not leave her bedroom, and then, of course, her perimeter was reduced to the circumference around her bed so that then her bed itself became her universe. This sort of extreme agoraphobic symptom is not unlike that of Howard Hughes, the billionaire who eventually would not or could not leave his bed.

Although knowing the symptom-code and feeling certain that applying it could produce some insight, for sure, it's use could not cure this hugely dense symptom. The symptom itself was profoundly resistive to treatment and her hypothesized implosion of anger so very severe, that she was entirely and hopelessly infused with rage. The story she initially told, which she herself described as the problem, seemed indeed to be the problem.

Apparently, for the past 20 years, the duration of her employ, this woman had been having an affair with her very wealthy employer. When she first started working for this man she was about 40 years of age, and this was to be the first long-term relationship of her life. She reported having had several boyfriends, but all these past relationships were of short duration.

Her history implied that she was a very dependent person, having lived with a bachelor brother for the 10 year period prior to her bookkeeping job. At that time she had no real savings and lived month to month, spending all of her earnings for rent and other necessities. When the affair began, this man who was married with a family of his own, was 60 years old. Before the end of the first year of their liaison he purchased an apartment for her and there had her safely ensconced for the ensuing duration of their 20 year relationship. In addition, he continuously showered her with expensive clothing and jewelry, and as a bonus, generous cash gifts. Over the ensuing two decades, she invested much of that money and became affluent on her own.

Because he was so considerate as well as generous with her, she never believed he would terminate their relationship. Rather, it seemed that because she became financially independent, it would be she who could step away from the relationship. As it turned out, and in a psychological sense, she would never have been able to leave the relationship because she was so emotionally dependent on this man. She believed that the same need she had for him, he had for her. To whatever extent that may or may not have been true, eventually, and immediately preceding the point of the acute onset of her agoraphobic symptom, he had broken their tie.

At first, after he turned 80, he began to complain that rather than his schedule easing, it was becoming tighter, busier. Then he suddenly announced that he would be unable to see her as much. It was then that she started spending week-day evenings as well as weekends, alone. This was in contrast to how it had always been with them. In the past, for them to spend one weekend day and one or two evenings per week together, had become a tradition and this had continued throughout their relationship.

In addition, her bonuses stopped and he informed her that her job would be reduced to two days a week. Decreasing her visibility at the office was the partic-ular stimulus that crystallized her anger, – making it palpable. The other insults made her feel "bad, upset, disappointed, sad," but not consciously angry. Of course, these adjectives she used were all code words for anger, but she was not able to experience the anger. At first, she could only experience feeling "bad, upset, disappointed, and sad." Then she began to realize she was angry at him. All along, however, and unconsciously, she was most likely, raging against him. Yet she could not permit herself to be conscious of this rage because its very magni-tude would indicate to her that their relationship was really, in effect, no more.

The point about her minimal presence at the office felt to her as though he was going to incrementally decrease her presence to zero. This seemingly inexorable advance to zero was difficult for her to bear because, as she put it, "My only claim to fame was that everyone at the office knew I was important." Apparently, all the employees knew that she was the boss' "special friend," and so they all deferred to her, and for those two decades she was treated like royalty. This was the only period of her life that she felt special, despite the fact that she was special only insofar as she was illegitimate royalty. Her employer never intended to leave his wife and family and always told her so. She accepted the arrangement because as she herself said, "I knew I was never going to be married, and I never wanted to have children, so this was just perfect for me, and I loved him."

Applying the Symptom-Code

In this case, application of the symptom-code was quite simple. Her wish was a direct one, she wanted him to stay with her – a positive wish. Ultimately then, an increase in tension was experienced if there was any demand for her to leave her apartment, which for her could only mean that she would have to be in an envi-ronment, that in reality implied her "demise." The only cure for this increased tension was in the agoraphobic symptom; that is, gratification was gained if she did not leave the apartment. Her tension would be relieved if she obeyed the ago-raphobic mandate; remaining "closeted" therefore, was an absolute denial of what she felt was her horrible reality.

Second, as stated, it is assumed that she swallowed an enormous amount of rage and didn't know it except that she had a hint of this repressed rage when finally she learned that her job had been cut back. In this respect her humiliation was too conscious and she could not avoid recognizing it. Otherwise, as she indicated, she felt bad and sad and disappointed, anything but furious, and enraged. Thus, this woman used an entire glossary of anger synonyms or code words for anger rather than being conscious of her debilitating, volcanic inner devastation. Certainly, this kind of utter rejection assumes the presence of a maximum amount of repressed rage.

Third, the *who*, with whom she was enraged, was obviously her boss/lover. Knowing it did not at all have any salubrious effect on her. The fact was that her emotional dependency on this man was all-consuming. She herself could never have left him, and she knew that he was aware of this. In addition, it was he, who terminated the relationship in the abrupt, impersonal manner that she reported, and this was enough evidence to reveal quite a plausible rationale for her profound sense of diminishment. The result of it all was the appearance of a terrible symptom that was inaccessible to treatment.

It was a death. In a case with such intense dependency, the abrupt cessation of the dependent relationship could easily produce the kind of powerlessness, the kind of helplessness that generates intense rage, that in this case was initially managed by keeping the intense feelings unconscious, out of awareness. Thus, the agoraphobic symptom resulting in this woman's confinement to the perimeter around her bed was equivalent to her death. She could not function without the dependent relationship. She was not alive without it, and for all intents and purposes, she was essentially acting out her death. The acting out, the agoraphobic symptom, was so acutely entrenched that it would seem that only one key could unlock it, and that key was not the symptom-code nor perhaps was it even the medication. The only key that would seem able to unlock the symptom was a reconstituted and secure dependent relationship.

Thus, if her lover would suddenly appear at her bed, and tell her that it was all a mistake, that the relationship would continue to be how it always was, and that most importantly, she could, of course, return to her job full-time, then it is assumed that her sense of self-esteem would instantly return and like magic, she would surely recover her bearings; especially with the realization that her royal privileges still obtained. Only then, would she permit herself to be cured and only then would she be able to cross *The Line* into a *doing* reality place and out of her deadly withdrawal. It was not to be.

Chapter 17
Chaos: A Case of Compulsive Collecting and Hoarding

A 55-year-old man had been collecting disability insurance since his accident in a machine shop some years earlier. He had slipped on an oil spill and eventually needed back surgery. He never again had a salaried job. However, he was exceedingly happy with his avocation. He fancied himself a master craftsman.

He lived with his wife and 15 year old daughter in a house that his wife had purchased with inherited funds. His wife and daughter were attentive to him. However, they were really pitying him and trying to shore him up, to reassure him, to strengthen his ego. The real problem they faced was that he was a collector and hoarder. Further, although he knew how to build things, he was never able to finish a project, and so there were half-chairs, and half-cabinets, and so forth, strewn all over the house. The problem was so severe that the daughter could never have friends over because the scene was quite bizarre.

This was the case of an obsessive-compulsive disorder, with an emphasis on the compulsion, almost certainly masking deeper pathology. His penchant for amassing clutter was based on his notion that whatever tool or stray piece of wood he would come across, could possibly be useful to him in his work. Thus, over more than a decade, the house was loaded with junk. Apparently, not a single surface was available on which even to place a saucer.

His wife was at her wits end, and threatened to leave him unless he sought treatment. She reasoned with him, trying to appeal to logic, saying to him that of course he knew that he never finished making even a single piece of furniture. Everything was always in the process of becoming. In response, he would acknowledge that she was right, but insisted that his plan was also always to get to each project and indeed, finish it, but he never did. His capacity for rationalization and denial was immense, and his ability to amass clutter–hundreds, even thousands of tools, as well as wood strips, planks, partitions, and random wood objects–was world class. Even he was beginning to see that the rooms in the house were filling up. Yet, this didn't prevent him from collecting and amassing new supplies each day. When his wife threatened to leave, and despite the fact that it motivated him to seek treatment, he was also rather of two minds about his wife leaving home because as he finally said, "It was embarrassing for me to have her live in that, and for her to see it every minute."

Thus, this man knew how crazy the whole thing was, but knowing was not sufficient to motivate him to do something about it. Rather, his feeling held sway and it was this feeling of needing to do "it" that transcended any intellectual knowing. The fact was, that this chaotic clutter collecting, was a severe symptom of compulsive hoarding.

His tendency to save (hoard) things began as early as he could remember. He always felt that to have "it," or to save "it," felt good. The "it," changed from time to time, but sometime in his late 30's, when he began to feel good about tools, this compulsive hoarding symptom flowered into a life's work. He reported that at times he felt "a little pressure" and when that happened, any tool he could find or buy, made him feel better. He just loved collecting them. Along with this compulsive penchant for curing his "pressure" by collecting tools, by his early 40's he also began collecting wood objects that he planned to utilize in his furniture projects.

After a while, his wife would comb through the various and sundry items and dispose of duplicates. This would anger him, but he was able to let it pass. It reminded him of what his mother would do when he was a child and his room became too cluttered. From time to time, he would arrive home from school, and his mother would have cleaned it all up and actually thrown much of it away. This would always infuriate him but he was too young and couldn't persuade her not to do it.

As the youngest of three siblings (two older sisters), with a span of 12 years between him and the middle sibling, given his baby status in the family, it might be expected that he would have been overprotected and overfed. However, what happened was that he was underfed, undersupervised, and relatively unattended.

In addition, in his growing-up years, the patient reported feeling alone much of the time. He was most at peace when he created games for himself and, as he said, "collected things." He claimed his mother would always insist on getting her own way and that his father was weak. He reported also that his father was kind to him but was controlled by his mother so that "he was never able to stand up to her, and I always hated his weakness."

For the most part, he indicated that he felt his parents favored his sisters. "No one talked to me," he said. He also indicated that he never felt entitled to anything and grew up with "a humongous inferiority complex." His response to feeling inadequate, unentitled, and not a bona fide family member, was to develop expertise in various areas. For example, he was a good artist and apparently would spend almost all of his time drawing and painting. He also learned how to build things and became proficient with tools. But from an early point on, he began noticing that he wouldn't finish things and that he procrastinated. This was especially true in school, when he would be perennially late handing in homework as well as papers that he needed to write. He also noticed that he was "anxious a lot of the time," and eventually, he dropped out of high school.

Applying the Symptom-Code

The diagnostic picture indicates an obsessive-compulsive pattern with an emphasis on compulsive behavior. Deeper pathology is a virtual certainty, and because the symptom was so entrenched and had become so characteristic of him, psychotherapy alone, in the absence of medication, was likely to be an exercise in futility. Similarly, use of the symptom-code would not be able to aid in resolving his conflict and curing the symptom.

The compulsive behavior of collecting and hoarding relieved his tension. Whenever he began to feel tense, he looked for things to bring home. If he found something, a tool, or some wood, then he felt better, treating his tension by acquiring treasures that essentially acted as medication. His act of collecting, therefore, along with the obsessive idea he got of keeping it, successfully reduced his tension and gave him comfort.

Of course, the reduction of tension by the compulsive act never solved the problem, or ever cured the symptom. Rather, when the tension began to build again, then he needed to repeat the pattern. The net result of all of this repetition compulsion, was the ultimate saturation of all space in his living environment with his tools, his wood, and his furniture in various stages of development.

This compulsive hoarding symptom was of a chronic nature. The symptom usurped the main frame of his personality, and in so characteristic a manner that the symptom had insinuated itself into his personality-trait repertoire, and become, a symptom-trait and not merely an isolated compartmentalized symptom sitting apart from his trait structure. The symptom was not accessible to talk therapy solely, and required a medication regimen along with psychotherapy.

With respect to the symptom-code, it must be assumed that he had repressed a great deal of anger, and that this repression originally occurred in childhood, presumably in response to his insecure sense of place in the family, perhaps in response to his belief that he really didn't have a place in the family, or with some other still unknown dynamic factor of his life.

His parents' insistence on the legitimacy of their needs and his feeling that there existed an absence of legitimacy with respect to his needs, suggests a genesis for the ostensible repression of this anger. It would necessarily mean that he was not feeling like a bona fide individual. Under such circumstances, during his childhood, and on the face of it, it could be assumed that for much of the time, he must have been very angry.

Thus with respect to the ingrained nature of his symptom, a likely identifiable candidate for the *who* could be one of his parents. Yet, he was never really able to confirm this assumption of one of his parents as a sole anger-provocateur. In addition, in assessing the entire family dynamic, it would seem that his basic wish was always to be a bona fide equal with his sisters and treated as a whole person, a finished product. As it turned out, this wish seems to have been severely restricted, severely thwarted. In his adult life, he also seemed to feel quite unentitled, and in fact, left everything, all of his projects, in an unfinished state.

Of course the qualifier in any such case is that the entire psychodynamic picture is just an imposition of theory, and that this sort of difficulty – collecting, hoarding, as well as all other such life-long difficulty – may really be an example of a genetic or organic brain anomaly that expresses itself this way.

Taken together, his hoarding and his compulsive tension-reduction technique of collecting, may have offered him a symbolic solution to his problem. The more he collected and saved, the more his possessions increased and correspondingly, the more solid he could feel. In addition, it is possible that all of his unfinished projects perhaps served the purpose of creating the condition where the anticipation of finishing something and making it whole, meant that possibly he too could be bona fide and whole.

Of course, this kind of repetition-compulsion of collecting and hoarding could never make him bona fide and legitimate. Perhaps an examination of his early history, an analysis and working through of his early sense of not belonging, and a look at what he experienced as emotional and affectional exile, could help address his core conflict. With the addition of medication, it is possible that the compulsive behavior could entirely disappear. It would then be more possible for him to work on, and at least to talk about and examine, these formative influences that, it is assumed, were sustained in his unconscious, plaguing him his entire life.

Since his ostensible wish was a positive and direct one–to be accepted as one equal to his siblings, to possess a sense of legitimacy–then his symptom of compulsive collecting relieved his tension. Nevertheless, this particular problem, his symptom of compulsivity and hoarding, as well as the diagnostic implication of deeper psychotic (or brain) pathology, rendered this man unable to conduct his life in a normal manner. He had been unable to work for many years (notwithstanding his accident), and had been effectively unemployable mostly because, even at his job, complaints were heard about his lateness and failure to complete work.

It may be assumed that this man's predominant wish in childhood was to be accepted and that this wish was thwarted. It also may be possible to assume that he reflexively became angry at what he may have experienced as a sustained disempowerment regarding this dominant thwarted wish. In such a situation where he may have felt unentitled and not bona fide, it could be predicted that his anger, rather than becoming directly expressed, would probably become repressed and that the repression would have created the symptom. Thus, the issue was, what did his symptom mean, what did it symbolize?

The amassing and filling the house with compulsively collected tools and wood, and the hoarding of such material, leads to a rather simple symbolic connection of symptom and wish. That is to say, it might be hypothesized that he wanted to fix it all. He wanted to fix the family and fix himself; tools and wood, build something good. But alas, it all remained unfinished, behind *The Line* in withdrawal-wood, tools, and him. The wish was good, to repair his experience, but as a symptom destined to remain unfulfilled.

Chapter 18
"Not Thin Enough!":
A Case of Anorexia

A 28-year-old woman was hospitalized by her family after she made good on her promise, "Maybe suicide will work for me." She was found partly conscious in the family garage, locked in the closed car, with the engine running. It was considered a serious suicide attempt and not merely a gesture. It was absolutely clear that had she not been discovered in time, she would have died.

This woman was an only child, and had been anorectic, more or less, for the past 13 years, since her mid adolescence, starting at about the age of 15. Hers was a rather typical anorexia in which she constantly fretted about her weight, pushed food away, weighed herself frequently, and for years, repeated her mantra: "Not thin enough!"

Along with her fetish of thinness, she had been somewhat withdrawn, dating also from her mid adolescence. The diagnosis arrived at in this, her first ever hospitalization, was depression with chronic anorexia and high suicide risk.

This kind of chronic anorexia along with her history of withdrawal, signaled that hers was a clinical syndrome that would be resistive to treatment, and the anorexia symptom itself was in all likelihood an inaccessible symptom, considered to be, more or less, incurable with known existing talk-treatment technology. Obviously, in such a case, various medication regimens would be tried in the hope of hitting upon some miracle agent or combination of agents.

The patient stated that her most important relationship was with her mother and that she never really took her father seriously. "He's weak," she said. "We patronize him, and that's about it." Her mother was the major power in her life, and she indicated that she talked everything over with her mother, including sexual matters.

When her mother was interviewed, the first thing she said was that her daughter hated to chew. The mother said that her daughter had never been withdrawn or demonstrated any bizarre or unusual behavior in childhood. But from childhood her daughter had been finicky over food, although, not anorectic.

In trying to identify some recent pivotal event that immediately preceded her suicide attempt, as well as fix on some person associated with such an event, the patient denied any such possible specific causative stimuli. However, in continuing to trace her history from the present to the recent past, and then to the more distant past, the patient happened to reveal that she had not gotten her period for almost the entire past year, about eight months. In reviewing what may have happened eight months prior to her suicide attempt and hospitalization, she revealed that she had an emotionally draining experience. She had been heartbroken because a man she had met, who she felt liked her, and whom she very much liked, rejected her because he actually told her she was "skin and bone," and that he "couldn't do it." He was harshly direct with her and told her he didn't like to lie, so that was how he felt. She was just "too thin." Interestingly enough, although this man told her she was too thin, her own incessant refrain for the past half of her life was, "Not thin enough!"

When her mother was asked about the patient's failed relationship with this man, she indicated that the end scene was quite horrible and confirmed that her daughter had felt terribly heartbroken over the rejection. Apparently, the patient spent the remaining months pining for the absent partner, and it seemed to her mother that she had not gotten over it and that, again, according to the mother, this rejection may have been "the cause of all of her trouble." It also seemed likely, based upon the correlation of events, that the patient's current menstrual inhibition (amenorrhea), was fortified by this rejection trauma.

At first the patient was reluctant and even in protest about discussing her feelings regarding this failed relationship, and especially with respect to the fact that she was terribly hurt by it. When she did finally discuss it, a torrent of emotion erupted. She cried and admitted to feeling devastated by the experience. Part of her distress concerned a wish on her part to look good for this man, yet she constantly felt that despite his desire for her to gain weight, she was not thin enough. Her answer obeyed a more compelling personal inner demand, and therefore, by default, she dismissed his feelings. Thus, rather than comply with his wishes by gaining weight, she obeyed those personal inner commands of hers, unconscious though they certainly were, and continued to avidly work at actually losing more weight and therefore, getting thinner.

This woman harbored ambivalent feelings about her mother. She felt that she needed her mother's blessings for all sorts of daily decisions, as well as for emotional support, and simultaneously she resented that she could only feel good when she had won her mother's approval. Any question posed to her about the pivotal condition that ignited a suicidal impulse in her was met with a studied silence. She would stare but not answer. Finally she admitted that a friend of hers had told her that this man, about whom she was agonizing, was engaged and was soon to be married. It was then, she finally confessed, that she decided to kill herself.

Apparently, this woman had developed an entire fantasy life involving this man, and in the process of developing her fantasy, had decided that he would change his mind and would be in touch with her. This thought would make her feel better, and it was just about the only thing that in fact, could make her feel better. She indicated that when her friend had told her about his impending marriage, she felt "everything crashing down," – that she really had nothing to live for. According to her mother, at that time, she became embroiled in an argument with her parents and shouted: "Nothing works for me. I've tried everything but suicide. Maybe suicide will work for me." In any event, her parents had not taken what she said about trying suicide as a serious threat. They only understood it as a figure of speech and an hysterical verbal lashing out.

Thus, the two issues that became at least somewhat clear in the distillation of her history, in her interviews, as well as in the interviews with her mother, were: (1) that she was exceedingly hurt by the man who rejected her; and, (2) that the relationship with her mother contained strong dependency features on the patient's part, along with an imputation of power on the mother's part. Whether or not her mother had personal needs to control everything around her, or whether by default, the mother was endowed with such power by her daughter, nevertheless, the patient was infantilized within the family. This family constellation consisted of a powerful mother, an ineffectual father, and the patient herself, an infantilized, somewhat regressed only child, who had grown up to be a dependent woman.

Applying the Symptom-Code

The anorectic syndrome, along with her suicide attempt, were the most dramatic components of this patient's behavior, but which was the symptom, the anorexia or her suicide attempt? The suicide attempt could not be considered the symptom because it was an impulsive act that she could have modified at any time during the process. Even if it were a carefully and thoughtfully planned attempt, nevertheless, she could have controlled it.

On the other hand, her anorexia was not something she could control. It was habituated, and it was a consistently expressed part of her personality. In fact, the anorexia had so embedded itself in her personality that it could be considered the type of symptom that swallows the person whole, and then the personality becomes the symptom. In this sense, the patient's entire life, her personality, and the organization of her life, literally revolved around her anorexia, which had become a symptom-trait.

In such cases, treatment and cure of the symptom solely by psychotherapy is quite problematic. Nevertheless, the symptom-code can be applied here in order to examine the constituents of her symptom, also with an eye toward seeing how the symptom cohered, and perhaps, and with some speculation, as to why it had become so entrenched.

Focusing strictly on her anorexia and not on her suicide attempt, it would be most likely that the *who* in her life was her mother. This would necessarily mean that she was angry at her mother, repressed the anger, and what emerged from her unconscious conflict about this anger toward her mother, was the symptom of anorexia. But how did the anorexia symptom become a neurotic product the purpose of which was to satisfy her basic wish, albeit in this perverse form, as anorexia?

The answer to this question requires a guess as to her basic wish. Given the extent of her symptom, with all of its life-threatening implications, then it must be assumed that her anger toward her mother was of considerable strength. For one, her extreme dependency on her mother's approval would in all likelihood generate great anger. The principal upon which this proposition is based concerns the relation of dependency and anger insofar as *dependency always breeds anger.* Thus, because she always had been so dependent on her mother, she would certainly always have been angry at her, but at a deep unconscious level.

An example of the operation of such a principal can be seen in the psychology of the dependency of childhood giving way to the sturm und drang of adolescence. In addition to new hormonal activity in adolescence that usually causes such upset, nevertheless, the many years of childhood dependency, where reliance on parents is so great, also contributes to the outbreak of anger during adolescence. Second, there were intimations in this case, that the patient's mother was a controlling type. Assuming the truth of this impression, then a strong potential for anger in the daughter, would also surely be a possibility. Third, the severity of the symptom also suggests that a great store of anger was being unconsciously sustained.

It would be easy to assume that because of the dependency problem in this woman her basic wish was to become more autonomous, more independent, more mature. Yet, it might be that the nature of the anorectic symptom implies something different. Since the dependence on the mother was so strong, and since this implies that the repressed anger in this woman was similarly strong, then it may have been that this woman's wish was an indirect, negative one–an avoidant wish. The wish may have been targeted at her needing to reduce the tension generated by the anger; that is, the wish would be not to be angry. In this sense, the wish would be that the anger somehow would become less intense, and not be so pervasive. This sort of indirect wish indicates that the symptom, in this case of anorexia, can never relieve tension; that is, the indirect wish would produce a painful symptom and not one that relieves tension–"Damn it, not thin enough!" It is this kind of indirect avoidant wish that reveals what the anorectic symptom really says.

What Does the Anorectic Symptom Really Say?

If the anorectic symptom could talk what would it say? We know that first, consciously, the symptom in the voice of the patient says: "Not thin enough!" But this observation is really a translation from another underlying language, the language of repression, of the unconscious. Thus, when the patient looks at her reflection in the mirror, to her eye her image is not pleasant. She thinks, "Not thin enough!" So she tries to lose even more weight, all the while, day in and day out, agonizing about how it's never enough.

The point is, no matter how much weight she loses, her eyes see "Not thin enough!" But what is it that she is *really* saying? The answer seems to be that whenever she looks at her reflection in the mirror and sees "Not thin enough!" she is really seeing, and saying to herself, while of course, not realizing it: "The anger is still there!" The further, and even more salient point here is that one cannot dilute or rid oneself of anger by getting thinner. However, since an unconscious equivalence has been construed between anger and thinness, then if one wants to reduce anger one then goes ahead and reduces weight, tries to get thinner. Of course, in reality, thinness and anger have no seeming discernible relation, no significant correlation. Yet, once such a symbolic equivalence is established, there forms an inextricable unconscious cause and effect relationship between getting thinner and reducing anger. The problem is that this cause and effect relationship is just that, a symbolic, unconscious, and strictly behind *The Line* construction. It is a construction based on distortions, on unfulfilled needs, and on constraints that the person feels, the solution to which is to create fantasy connections of cause and effect–in this case, *thinning* out her anger. These, or course, are behind *The Line* connections, connections made in withdrawal, that have virtually nothing to do with real cause and effect but can become so powerful that such fantasy distortion can constitute a path to personal destruction.

Thus, this woman's anorectic symptom, about which she says, "Not thin enough!" strongly implies that her reservoir of unconscious, repressed anger is intense and deep, and that it is putting tremendous pressure on her. In an attempt to reduce the pressure, she reduces her weight but alas, the anger remains untouched. For an anorectic person to try to reduce the magnitude of the anger by losing weight and of course fail at it, and then need to lose more weight, and become even thinner, and then again not have it work, would most likely produce a secondary anger which would then be a result of poor performance–actually, failure. One anger on top of another is what becomes typical, so that this kind of symptom would in this way be fortified, reinforced, and then neurotically and consistently nourished. So, rather than the nourishment of the person, we get a nourished symptom!

Despite the fact that such a symptom is so entrenched, nevertheless the use of medication to neutralize some of the anger can be very helpful, and in addition, perhaps can help provide access to the symptom via psychotherapy. Yet, in its present form, this anorectic symptom would most likely be inaccessible solely to therapy. In addition, in this case the symptom was of a chronic nature so that the prognosis for an efficient recovery strictly on the basis of psychotherapy was guarded.

With respect to her suicide attempt, we may assume that her almost-romance with the man who crushingly rejected her also felt as though it was her only chance of liberation from a nuclear dependency on her mother which she ambivalently both wanted and did not want, and this hope was resoundingly dashed. But liberated from what, from whom? Would she be liberated from her mother, and directly into the arms of another figure upon whom she would again depend? The hope was a false one. Her suicide attempt thus was possibly based upon another behind *The Line* hope resting on the assumption that if only the relationship with this man worked, then she would have achieved her love aim and, in addition, become liberated from a life of infantile, regressive dependency on her childhood parental figure. Paradoxically, however, this may have been only half her wish–the other half perhaps being a need to remain dependent on this self-same childhood parental figure.

Based upon this plethora of assumptions, hypotheses, and propositions, the diagnosis of this woman also needs to consider several other factors: withdrawal greater than that originally assumed; wishes that may have become overly persuaded by a form of thinking that confused correlation with causation; and a suicidal despair based less on the actual breakup of her relationship with her man friend, and more on a distorted sense of issues related to her autonomy.

With respect to treatment issues, psychotherapy could be exceedingly useful, assuming an effective regimen of medication, both to address the anorexia and the depressive elements of her personality, as well as to address the ostensible presence of deep reserves of anger. Importantly, it would be necessary to pry loose the distorted connection she presumably has made between anger and thinness. Therefore, psychotherapy would offer her a chance to better align her thinking, to encourage more independent action, and of course, also to lift repression, especially that of anger, or as Freud counseled, to make the unconscious, conscious.

Chapter 19
Dissociative Identity Disorder: A Case of "Split Personality"

A 35-year-old man had been hospitalized for the second time in one year, for major depression and withdrawal. Shortly after each hospitalization, the depression seemed to lift, and it was thought that even without medication, these hospitalizations tended to revitalize him. The second hospitalization was at a state mental institution.

He worked as a handyman to clients whom his adoptive mother cared for in her capacity as a home nurse's aide. This arrangement apparently had been successful for them over a period of many years. The patient would become agitated when discussing this mother-son arrangement primarily because, when she was working, he felt deprived, actually bereft over his separation from her. Yet, it was this mother who convinced the patient to admit himself to the hospital, and whose requests, he confessed, he could not refuse.

At first, his diagnosis was easily decided upon because he demonstrated each of the main constituent properties of depression. Yet, before any medication was even ordered, his depression lifted. At the same time, however, he had managed to acquire as well as conceal, some women's toiletries, cosmetics, and clothing—panties, padded bra, blouse and short leather skirt. He was eventually apprehended by hospital security after they found him changing from female clothing into his shirt and pants. His problem was that he didn't have time to dispose of the female garb he was wearing. He did, however, manage to wipe off his lipstick and rouge. After a chase, he was found in his hospital room with a jar of cold cream in his hands, paper towels smeared with lipstick, and female clothing strewn on his bed. He was being pursued by hospital security after it was reported that a man in women's clothing was exposing himself in full view of the windows of one of the buildings housing female patients. He had been exhibiting himself while in full female regalia.

When he was apprehended for exhibitionism, he was not at all depressed. An astounding part to the story was that this man was 6 feet 4 inches tall, was a lithe mesomorph, and was handsome and charming. On the negative side, he had a child like innocence about him. Nevertheless, when he was apprehended, a padded bra, a blouse, and a blonde wig with shoulder length curls, were found under the covers of the bed.

It was reported by the women who saw him, that he had pulled up the leather skirt he was wearing, to reveal his genitals. He was apparently fully erect. Yet he denied ever having anything to do with these female items, and could not explain how they happened to be there, on and in his bed. In scouring his room, hospital security also discovered a diary in his bureau drawer. The diary was essentially a conversation; one person, a man, talking to another, a woman. In the diary, the man explained to the woman that he felt good only when attacking others, while the woman, in answering him, explained that she only felt good when exhibiting her penis. And the diary went on like that, one or two pages from him to her, and then one or two pages from her to him.

The patient denied knowing anything about the diary, and in fact, his script was different from the script of the other two in the diary. However, evidence against him began to mount when, along with some of the female patients' positive identification of him as the exhibitionist, a male patient complained that he was almost attacked by our patient for no reason that he could see, and that then our patient was often in a foul mood, scornful and smoldering, and always, it seemed, looking for a fight.

This unusual patient who was at first obviously under diagnosed as only depressed, was presented at a staff conference, and in the face of patently clear evidence, denied ever exhibiting himself. He also denied ever feeling aggressive toward others, also here again, even in the face of eyewitness accounts. Yet, his denials were seemingly authentic, and therefore, believable.

Thus, it was felt that his actual diagnosis, although certainly, at least containing an episodic depressive condition, was deeper, more extensive, and implied a more serious complex of variables. This more complex syndrome qualified as a classic case of dissociative identity disorder, formerly known as multiple personality, and before that, referred to in the professional nomenclature as, split personality. The depression was then seen as secondary to the fuller picture of this possible diagnosis of dissociative identity disorder.

After some time it became evident that his only visitor was his adoptive mother, who it seemed was rather inappropriate in her demeanor. She was in her mid 50's. She had adopted the patient when he was 3 years old. She divorced soon thereafter and retained custody of him.

Her inappropriate demeanor consisted of a rather garish display of her figure–both with respect to style of clothing and color. She was a vividly voluptuous woman who wore shockingly bright clothing of a cut that would display her figure to what she considered to be its best advantage. She admitted that the patient cross-dressed and often even exhibited himself to her. She dismissed this as: "Some people do this and some do that–everyone has something strange about them. He's basically harmless."

The patient only gave scant information about his life and was uniformly general in his descriptions. His only interest, it seemed, was in describing his adoptive mother, whom he called "beautiful." He would regale staff personnel with stories of how beautiful she really was, and it became clear that his only focus of interest was on her.

Basic Formation of the Dissociative Identity Disorder (Split Personality)

First, the dissociative identity disordered person is one who usually houses two basic personalities other than the usual self, referred to as the host. Of the other two personalities, one is aggressive and the other sexual. Theoretically, it is supposed that because aggression and sex were made difficult, or even impossible to integrate into the personality, the subject needed then to compartmentalize these components into two other basic personalities. Reasons for the difficulty in integrating the components of aggression and sex into the personality usually have been attributed to early abuse. The abuse discussed, it is thought, revolves around physical abuse, meaning hostile and aggressive beatings and the like. Yet, it is also thought that an early co-opting of sexual favors can lead to similar consequences. It is often the case that an incestuous parent can create a sense in the child of feeling excluded from normal family life–actually to feel exiled, outside the normal perimeter and parameters of family life, even though they still remain physically within the family.

Further, the alter personalities can know of one another and of the host, whereas the host personality, in a classic case of the "split," never knows of the existence of the other two. It is in this sense, that each alter develops its own memories, emotions, personality style, even handwriting. In this way, the trauma experienced by the subject during childhood duress can be partialed out of the person's consciousness, thus nullifying the psychological pain of such presumed trauma.

The self, in such a personality constellation, becomes fractured, thereby making this kind of symptom extraordinarily difficult to treat. It should also be noted that despite the framing of this condition as a diagnosis, the multiple personality organization is definitely also a symptom, albeit, an all encompassing one. It is the kind of symptom that swallows up the person whole, and it then becomes difficult to see the person as different from the symptom. It is a case in which, in essence, the person becomes the symptom.

As the host personality develops other alters–as many as 100 have been reported–they can all be variations on the two major themes of aggression and sex. These other alters can be suspicious, narcissistic, or even of opposite genders. They can also take on aspects of child behavior, and any number of other variables can determine the nature of the alter. However, it is probably the case that all of them will be derivatives of the aggressive and sexual personas.

The shift that alters make from one to the other, is called *switching*, and the range of consciousness that the host person can have of the others, can be, at one pole, nothing at all, and at the other, some consciousness of the others. It is thought that the purpose of this kind of psychic fracture is to disconnect from painful memories, or even from excruciatingly embarrassing memories. Of course, connected to these memories would be emotions and attitudes that correspondingly are also parsed, compartmentalized, as it were, and placed outside of the host's consciousness.

Secondary diagnoses or attendant symptoms along with the main diagnosis of dissociative identity disorder, can consist of an entire range of typical psychological and emotional difficulties. These can include depression, as with the patient discussed here, lability of mood, any number of phobias, psychotic symptoms such as delusions, intrusive thoughts, and obsessions and compulsions, to list a sample of such standard psychiatric symptoms.

Applying the Symptom-Code

The patient presented here, in many ways, satisfies most of the criteria for the diagnosis of dissociative identity disorder. He exhibited the classic tripartite personality configuration of a host personality housing also an aggressive type and a sexual one. Despite his age, he was inextricably tied to his mother in a strikingly dependent relationship. In her visits to him, his mother was so inappropriately sexual and seductive, that to make the supposition that she was an oedipal seductress during his childhood, would not be far-fetched. Assuming this was so, the prediction of the effect of the severity of such disturbance can be more than mere conjecture.

Since he proclaimed no other relationships that meant anything to him, except the one with his mother, it again would not be far-fetched to assume that she was the *who*, and, by implication, that he had indeed harbored repressed anger toward her. This, by definition, must be so, because the underpinning of the symptom-code posits that without repressed anger, there can be no symptom. Perhaps, if he was in fact seduced by her, and indeed felt abnormal because of it, it would not be unusual for him then to always have been angry at her, and especially never to have known it. We must ask two questions: What was his wish, and how does the symptom of his disordered identity gratify that wish?

According to theory, rather than not feeling the human emotions of aggression and sex at all, his fractured personality could have been an ingenious psychic arrangement enabling him to configure separate compartments for these emotions. Thus, his wish probably was indeed to be able to have aggressive and sexual feelings even though, ostensibly, there was an outside force prohibiting it. In cult groups, for example, the leader usually controls aggression and sex, and followers are bound by such control. It may be that control of this patient by a sexually deranged parent resulted in the same sort of conflict regarding the control of sex and aggression that brought about his particular personality kaleidoscope.

Thus, so that he could be whole, his wish likely could have been to contain both aggressive and sexual feelings in his personality. Since in the symptom-code, a positive, direct wish generates a symptom that relieves tension, then such an inference is rather confirmed by the fact that in the split personality, this dissociative identity disordered person, the full expression of whatever is the alter personality, feels good. The distinct alter, therefore, is a pure expression of its essence, sometimes aggressive and sometimes sexual, and sometimes a variant of these, all of which, reduce tension.

In the case of this patient, when he occupied the sexual exhibitionistic alter role, exhibiting himself gave him pleasure, and he also felt good when in the aggressive role, he could expostulate his anger in aggressive acts. Thus, his wish was gratified by an organization of personality that housed three separate aspects of his needs. The first was the host, a nice, if rather innocent man; the second, a rather argumentative and aggressive person; and the third, a highly sexualized cross-dressing exhibitionist.

His cross-dressing is also interesting because often in such cases, the cross-dresser needs to disguise his manliness before he can assert it–a double dose of disguise, as it were. The data concerning his relationship with his mother also reflected strong dependency along with an inability to refuse her anything. This sort of relationship could, of course, contain imperatives concerning some covert instruction for him to remain child like, thereby denying any overt masculine sexual maturity. In such a case, it could be hypothesized that his exhibitionism would, actually and ingeniously, only occur in female form.

Of course, the entire syndrome here is a bold example of a behind *The Line* scenario where this man existed most of the time in fantasy–albeit extensive fantasy, in roles acted out with meticulous care. His story and his acting out of these roles is particularly poignant, especially when viewed from the vantage point of his diary. The diary seems to have been a profound example of his loneliness. It created for him the ability to have friends–both of his alters had become friends, and had begun writing to one another. Despite the fact that he claimed he knew nothing of this relationship between them, nevertheless he was the author of their relationship and therefore, on an unconscious level he was deriving some gratification from their kinship.

This is not the kind of symptom that can be cured with the simple application of the symptom-code. With respect to treatment, a delicate, gradual accommodation would have to be made between his alters and himself, the host. This would necessarily constitute a rapprochement among all of them, accomplished through dialogue. He would have to get together with them, to talk about them, even perhaps, with them. Most of all, the apparent prohibition against integrating these motifs of aggression and sex into his personality would need to be investigated, and the distortions about their dangers would have to be resolved. In addition, it may be expected that for him to become conscious of this inner drama, necessarily he would need to become more conscious of the experiences that were presumably repressed.

The original problem may concern his anger regarding the entire circumstance of the hypothesized cooption in his early life. Despite the presumed trade-off he made, that of giving up sex and aggression so that he could have his *wish* (exclusive rights to his adoptive mother and her likely seductions), nevertheless, for him to have developed such a complex symptom picture, points to an enormous amount of repressed anger toward this *who*.

The key to the entire picture therefore, seems to be an ostensible repressed anger toward his adoptive mother. This may be what is repressed in the deepest psychological sense, and at some point, along with other therapeutic work, would need to be made conscious in order to create for this person a new synthesis regarding a possible transformation of a fractured self into a whole one.

Chapter 20
An Asperger's Mind:
An Examination of the Case
of Nobelian John Forbes Nash, Jr.

A biography of the Nobel Prize winner John Forbes Nash, Jr. was written by Sylvia Nasar and published in 1998. The book, *A Beautiful Mind* won a National Book Critics Circle Award for biography, and a film based on the book, was also an Academy Award winner.

Dr. Nash was, by all accounts, considered to be a mathematician of genius whose intuitive abilities as well as his knack of utilizing novel ways of solving seemingly insoluble problems, engendered accolades. He was also considered by his colleagues to be so extraordinarily special that for most of his professional life, and despite his incapacitated psychological/emotional condition, various institutions and many colleagues, bent over backwards to support him, subsidize him, and even offer him intellectual professional shelter within their respective institutions.

Many of his colleagues as well as others, recognized that he was at least, odd. Many attributed this odd quality to his idiosyncratic genius, and much of what was considered a social inappropriateness, was overlooked or forgiven or just tolerated. He was occasionally abrupt with others, or could not or would not look directly at the person he was talking to. He could say things, quite unselfconsciously, that were so rudely direct as to embarrass, hurt the other person's feelings. For example, during a period when Professor Nash was trying to reconcile with his out-of-wedlock son, John David Stier, whom he had for the longest time neglected, Nash became critical of him suggesting that John David's profession of nursing was less than a stellar achievement, and that what he should really do is go to medical school. Further, Nash also suggested that it might be a good idea for John David to look after, and care for, John David's younger half-brother, John Charles, who was Nash's legitimate Ph.D. mathematician son, who was schizophrenic. As reported by Nasar in *A Beautiful Mind,* instead of trying to harmonize his own proposed union of the half-brothers, Nash, on second thought, then quite directly said to John David, that in reality he didn't think it would do his schizophrenic son any good to be around a "less intelligent older brother" – meaning John David, the son to whom he was talking.

This absence of empathy or strange relatedness, was typical of Nash. At best, these were genuine, authentic examples of a kind of socially aberrant understanding, and at worst, they could be considered examples of Nash as a socially challenged person based on a developmental arrest or particular developmental pathology. It is no doubt that Professor John Forbes Nash, Jr., whatever his true diagnosis, was, at least, socially challenged.

Along with this social awkwardness, Dr. Nash was also reported, as stated, to have difficulty in making eye contact with others, as well as not being very versatile in establishing peer relationships. Thus, his ability for emotional reciprocity was suspect. On a firmer foundation with respect to pathology, he was ultimately diagnosed with schizophrenia, along with manic-depressive illness. He displayed delusional thinking and experienced auditory hallucinations that plagued him for most of his adult life.

Diagnosis

Although indeed, Nash was afflicted with schizophrenia, as well as experiencing bouts of mania and depression, nevertheless, the vast amount of clinical evidence actually suggests a more relevant diagnosis–that of Asperger's syndrome. As a diagnosis Asperger's syndrome may be more relevant because it seems evident that the diagnosis of Asperger's underlies the more symptomatic elements of his schizophrenia, his mania and depression, as well as the oddities of his behavior noted throughout his life, by many of his family and acquaintances.

Asperger's Syndrome

In the 1940's, this syndrome was formulated by a Viennese pediatrician, Hans Asperger. It is now considered to be among the spectrum of pervasive developmental disorders (PDD), and many professional psychiatric personnel, consider it to reflect high- level autism with neurologically based implications.

Most Asperger individuals show deficits in several broad categories of functioning, although variations on these themes are also quite common. Deficits in social relatedness usually characterize one of these categories. Another concerns a rather restricted and narrow, yet entirely intense corridor of interest in some particular subject matter. With Nash, this laser-beam corridor of interest was mathematics.

Further, Asperger individuals are frequently found in professorial positions or in professions that imply above average I.Q., and they also frequently demonstrate great talents in one or another area of functioning. In childhood, these kinds of people do not make friends very easily, and are loners. They are, however, usually immersed very early on in whatever is their particular narrow interest. In John Nash's case, it was science in general and mathematics in particular that attracted his attention early on, and fully absorbed his time.

Such children seem to exclude everything else from their daily interactions and even their daily conversations. Also, many Asperger children will express an abiding interest in cars, trains, and other transportation venues. In Nash's case, it was math that transported him. Mathematics was the vehicle of his cerebral geography, his mind, that he utilized, to travel. It could be said that he was always on some math excursion. As a matter of fact, when later Nash became schizophrenic, he may have expressed this inner signal to travel by externalizing it, and actually doing it. He literally would traverse continents, seemingly quite impulsively. Of course, it could be that out of the tyranny of his delusional state, he did this traveling to and fro, often, and for reasons that seemed entirely woven out of the fabric of his delusions–his inner distortions, fantasies, and even hallucinations.

In many individuals with Asperger's syndrome, one sees either an evident timidity as a permanent character or personality trait, or an impulsive aggressiveness. In some cases, these polar opposites coexist. On the one hand, the person can be quite timid and this quality can take various forms; it can appear as humility, shyness, reticence, modesty, diffidence, and so forth. On the other hand, along with this cluster of timidity traits, there can also simultaneously exist an impulsivity, a narcissistic greed, and an aggressiveness. In Nash's case, it seems that both existed simultaneously. He was timid, shy, modest, even childlike, while also at times demonstrating belligerence, stridency, impulsivity, provocativeness, and aggression.

A hard-core characteristic in the diagnosis of Asperger's is an absence of delay in cognitive functioning, or language development, and the person easily shows the ability to work in his own interest. Certainly, Professor Nash met these required diagnostic conditions of Asperger's. In addition, and as stated, he exhibited certain social impairments, including a poor understanding of social cues, and, frequent inappropriate emotional responses. Thus, to diagnose him with a serious disorder of empathy seems justified because his response style could be defined as one in which the person suffers with such a sufficient absence of empathy.

Dr. Nash also had an iron-clad will that was governed certainly more by his internal signal than by any external reality cue. This willfulness, was imposed on others as much as it was self-imposed, and in addition, was a greater imperative of his personality than was any consideration of empathy toward others. In fact, later in life he was able to ignore the compelling force of his auditory hallucinations by sheer will-power. He refused to comply with those ever-present voices of his hallucinations. Only the willpower of an Asperger's mind would likely be able to accomplish this considerable emotional/cognitive feat.

With respect to language, rather than showing prosody difficulties–intonation, rate of speech, inflection–he was quite proficient in his use of language and could and would spontaneously create brilliant puns. He displayed excellent command of language, and just for the fun of it, even created several interesting strategic games.

Although, Asperger's is not considered curable, symptoms can become either greater or, less visible as the person ages. In addition, Asperger individuals often marry and have families. They are usually not terribly good at it, but with an understanding spouse, the marriage can be managed and even sustained, although under continued stress. Nash's marriage qualifies in this respect, although his wife, Alicia Larde Nash, eventually divorced him after almost a lifetime of such emotional and psychological stress, struggle, and strain, along with, it should be noted, extraordinary, even uxurious devotion.

The Proposed Deep Structure of Nash's Schizophrenia

Yes, John Forbes Nash, Jr. was schizophrenic, but, his schizophrenia was in all likelihood, an overlay to a highly probable basic Asperger condition. It was the Asperger's that was fundamental to his personality. All else, it is proposed was accompaniment, including any mania or depression.

Several questions beg to be asked. First, what was the pivotal event that triggered his first schizophrenic episode? Yes, there must have been a pivotal event! Second, who was the person involved in this pivotal event? Yes, there must be a *who* in the pivotal event! Third, what was Nash's purpose in becoming schizophrenic? Yes, there can be a purpose to the schizophrenia! Fourth, with respect to the symptom-code presented throughout this volume, what was his thwarted *wish*, and what can be deduced with respect to the assumption that, in order to develop this overlay of symptoms, he needed to *repress an enormous amount of anger and rage*? Yes, we can assume he had a thwarted *wish*, there was a *who*, and he did repress anger.

Dynamic Elements of Nash's Problem

It could be that the story begins with Nash's grandiosity. His particular brand of grandiosity seems to have contained two elements. The first, his genius in mathematics, was confirmed time and again, so that his notion of himself as a genius of great consequence had a solid grounding in reality. The second element concerned the extent of his grandiosity. It would seem that Nash wanted to be recognized, not only as a genius, but as *the* genius. There is evidence to believe that Nash's pathology with respect to grandiosity consisted of a classic megalomania, but because of the true extent of his genius, at least an aspect of his megalomania contained a profound non pejorative implication.

Among his many accomplishments were solutions to great and vexing problems both in pure and applied mathematics, and his method for understanding and solving such problems was recognized as unusually brilliant. For example, at one point he transformed nonlinear equations into linear ones and then solved the equations by non- linear measures. He would translate one language to another and then return to the original language in order to understand the deeper structure to the translation, ultimately solving the original problem. It is something like a painter taking a photograph of a painting and then doing a painting of the photograph in order to somehow animate the original work. In each transformation, interesting changes can be noted that perhaps then can reveal a different synthesis of the work. In addition, it's probably fun to do these transformations. At least by analogy, it is proposed that the great fun Nash had in life concerned his absorption in mathematical conundrums, the more complex, the better. It is as though his brilliance needed the very complex and most difficult challenges to stimulate his, and its, motivational juices. His ability to stay with a problem was remarkable. His attention was reflected in his persistent focus, and such problems, apparently without exception, evoked his intuitive powers. These challenges, and the promise of vanquishing them, or the anticipation of the moment when the solution would hit him, these expectations, seemed to nourish him. Nothing else seemed to matter as much.

And then there was the *Riemann*. The *Riemann Hypothesis* regarding prime numbers, was a problem of staggering proportions. It has been considered to be the most visible, perhaps outstanding problem in pure mathematics and theoretical physics, certainly successfully rivaling that of Fermat's Last Theorem, or even any proposed revision of quantum theory, which Nash, incidentally, also considered tackling. This hypothesis was proposed in the middle of the nineteenth-century by the great mathematician, George Friederich Beinhard Riemann. It was an attempt to unravel a deep truth about whole numbers. These prime numbers can only be divided by themselves, and they seem implicated in the puzzle concerning the reconciliation of Newtonian and quantum physics.

Thus, Nash's psychic investment was with the Riemann, and he decided to take it on. More accurately, it looks as though Nash decided not only that he would take it on, but that *he* would be the one to solve it! He tried every which way: by utilizing number systems; by applying logic of internal consistency; and, by other accounts, of even trying what some called, "wild approaches." If there ever could be a precipitator for Nash's schizophrenia, perhaps it would be the internally imposed pressure he would have been bound to experience in the pursuit of as important a problem as the Riemann, especially in the face of his failure to solve it.

But Nash did not become schizophrenic merely as a result of some kind of fracture in his psyche that broke him down; that would be too prosaic. No, a genius does genius things. And this genius perhaps may have been trying to solve the Riemann by *becoming* schizophrenic. He intuitively may have been trying to implement his intuition as he did with the transformation of nonlinear equations into linear ones, and then solving the problem by nonlinear measures. Thus, perhaps in this new schizophrenic thinking persona, he could do something that: (1) no one else had ever done, or perhaps would ever do; and (2) would then generate acclaim for doing something that would gain him a consensus as perhaps the greatest genius that ever lived-the ultimate confirmation of the validity and logic of his grandiosity. A megalomaniacal confirmation, with a hue even, as stated earlier, of the nonpejorative.

Such was his voracious focus on the Riemann. But alas, even in his translated, or transformed state, his schizophrenia, he couldn't do it, and he didn't do it-ever, or perhaps even, yet. He knew that others were working on it, and even before he became floridly schizophrenic, he knew who some of those others were. Once he was schizophrenic, however, and his psyche was therefore in its fractured state, even a person as singularly brilliant as John Forbes Nash, Jr. could not or would not, reconstitute himself. Delusions and hallucinations would then haunt him for years to come.

But even in his schizophrenic state, his struggle with a great problem like revising quantum theory or solving the Riemann, as well as his struggle with his megalomania was not over. He had also become incoherent and was exhibiting classic schizophrenic delusional thinking. Yet, even though his behavior seemed random and sick, nevertheless, it could be that all of it, all of his seemingly random, sick, pathological, paranoid, delusional thinking, revolved around, and made perfect sense, when viewed from the perspective of his ostensible megalomaniacal struggle with the great problem of the Riemann. There are many such examples of this struggle, but for the purpose of this exposition, two or three such examples should suffice.

The first example of the connection between his floridly schizophrenic symptoms and this presumed struggle with the Riemann, concerns Nash's obsessive and intrusive thoughts about seeing codes in newspapers and magazines. He would clip these articles and apparently plaster them all over his life. What he was doing was most likely using this delusion as a template in order to see the ostensible coded meanings from these articles. But what did this behavior really mean? One possible, and perhaps not very far-fetched hypothesis, is that his obsessive focus on newspapers (in order to receive their coded messages) was really an attempt to connect the coded messages to the solution of the Riemann. In fact, his repetitive, insatiable pursuit of these articles, and more importantly, the satisfaction this pursuit and these articles afforded him, indicated that getting these coded messages was his unconscious confirmation that he had indeed solved the Riemann, or was now about to. His basic wish was to solve the Riemann and his schizophrenic pathological musings and behaviors could likely have reflected a multitude of gratifications he derived each time he clipped an article or saw what he deemed to be a coded message. All of it could well have been about finally finding the solution to the Riemann. With all of these daily clippings, he could then solve it over and over again, a classic perseveration. And the concrete collection of these articles was his proof positive, that he was, in fact, doing it, and doing it, and doing it, solving it over and over.

Thus, all of his obsessional thinking as well as compulsive behavior regarding coded messages and clipping articles, rather than reflecting some random, crazy, and schizophrenic cognition, could now be seen as Nash's quite original and even brilliant solution to his conflict–an ingenious solution perhaps rivaling that of actually solving the Riemann. It possibly could be called *The Magnificent Nash Synthesis*.

This "Magnificent Nash Synthesis" would mean that the conflict no longer concerned the solution to the Riemann. Rather, his conflict was now resolved by figuring out a solution to *not* being able to solve the Riemann. In other words, Nash was so brilliant that because he couldn't solve the Riemann, then rather than solving it, he derived a way to solve the problem of *not* being able to solve it, and therefore, he was able to retain his megalomaniacal belief in his infallibility as a genius-the greatest genius.

What he may have done was to figure out a way to erase the Riemann as a problem by derealizing it. Assuming the validity of this conclusion, (tentative though it may be), the speculation here is that Nash's approach to erasing the Riemann, was to find the code in the magazine or newspaper, and clip the article. Article clipped-problem finished! This kind of solution to his conflict, given his schizophrenic condition, could be considered an overarching cognitive/organizational achievement, a feat of major proportion. Again, the problem was no longer the Riemann. The proof of his genius now, was that Nash had figured a way of retaining his grandiosity *because* he couldn't solve the Riemann. Thus, the greatest problem in mathematics was not the solution to the Riemann. The greatest problem in mathematics was in not solving it. Through a psychological transformation, Nash wins by not solving it.

As indicated, his initial answer to these supra and super cognitive/organizational achievements, was in the appearance of his transformed state, in the appearance of his schizophrenia. It may have been Nash's way to make something visible (in his schizophrenic state of seeing coded messages) that could perhaps not be visible in any normal thinking state. But he was not able to accomplish this intended goal of seeing some unusual path to the solution of the Riemann via his schizophrenic persona.

Thus, with respect to actually solving the Riemann, this schizophrenic transformation did not work. The only thing that worked was his Freudian acted out repetition-compulsion that never really mastered his anxiety. Rather, this repetition behavior only mastered his acting out of the conflict. In a practical sense then, in his schizophrenic state, his solution was to hear voices and become delusional about coded messages. And in these coded messages, was his perseverating solution to the Riemann. This was a schizophrenic perseveration of the first order, serving to gratify his need for a successful Riemann closure. Yet, this solution was enclosed in his even greater supra cognitive/organizational feat of erasing the Riemann altogether.

If this rather speculative scenario has some validity, then for him to remain schizophrenic would be an imperative in order to continue to disarm the grenade in his stomach at not really solving the Riemann. Remaining schizophrenic, therefore, was to control, erase, and solve the Riemann, all at the same time. An ingenious Nash paradox!

Another example of this kind of logic to the retention of his schizophrenia, to his unconscious organization, and to his confluence of thinking and behavior, also lending a kind of support to this theory of how Nash managed both to solve and to erase the Riemann, concerned his attempts to renounce his United Stated citizenship. He went to considerable lengths, over a long period of time, trying to do this. A possible answer as to why he would do so, again concerns his failure to solve the Riemann, along with another way of erasing the problem altogether. A possible hypothesis is that in his unconscious he could have posed an equation; that is, as a United States citizen, his mission was to solve the Riemann, which he wasn't able to do, so that naturally, to renounce his citizenship, could mean that he no longer felt the mandate to solve it, and therefore was off the hook. Thus, no mandate, no

Riemann, no agony. Under such a condition he could retain the full measure of his megalomania. "I am still the greatest genius," would be the surviving mantra because as a citizen of another world, the Riemann would not even exist!

A third hypothesis regarding his schizophrenia and its purpose, other than actually serving a compensatory need with respect to his actual failure in solving the Riemann, or to whatever extent a schizophrenic predisposition may have existed, concerns the relation between his basic presumed Asperger's state on the one hand, and the serious realistic challenge that he very likely experienced regarding his self-appointed megalomaniacal genius role, on the other. It must be realized that in Asperger functioning, despite the fact that such individuals can indeed have relationships with friends and family, the individual's basic relationship is with the self. When the experience as well as the belief tells the individual that a profound failure has occurred, a challenge emerges to this sort of narcissistic arrangement of the self. Thus, a challenge of the relationship of self to self is created. In the face of such a challenge, the Asperger individual has been forsaken. In this case, because of his failure to solve the Riemann, his grandiose self would have been subtracted from itself, and under such circumstances he would then have felt quite alone; feeling that perhaps he was not, and had never been the greatest genius he had hitherto believed himself to be. The problem is that in such a narcissistic, no less megalomaniacal Asperger's condition, when one is not the greatest, then one is nothing.

In Nash's case therefore, a truly remarkable and actually superbrilliant solution would have been for him to get a friend for his Asperger self. And that friend may well have been a schizophrenic one–John Forbes Nash, Jr., Asperger individual, in concert with John Forbes Nash, Jr., schizophrenic individual. If this is so, not only would it be that Nash is a mathematical genius, but for all intents and purposes, he would have to be considered a psychological one as well, notwithstanding the fact that the genius of his psychology would be to keep himself in a failure free state; that is, in a schizophrenic state with different citizenship, and therefore, of course, away from the Riemann.

Applying the Symptom-Code

The key here is identifying the *who* with whom Nash was, and perhaps still is, angry. We know that emotion must take an object, and that the object is always a person. Thus, he must be angry with a person. Or must he be? These axioms apply to individuals who are normally neurotic but do they apply to Asperger individuals? The answer seems likely to lie in a particular characteristic of the Asperger's symptom; that is the Asperger individual usually focuses on part-objects. Therefore, a theoretical half-step can be made, a fissure reveals itself, with respect to these axioms as they may apply to such Asperger individuals, namely, that inanimate objects are often personified. These inanimate objects are therefore subject to vitalization, to a symbolic animated existence usually, in part, as in part-object.

It is thus proposed, that this may have been the case with Nash and his intellectual, emotional, and psychological focus, or actual fusion with the Riemann. He personified the Riemann as though, quite naturally, it was a person. When he could not penetrate the problem of the Riemann, however, rather than becoming furious at the person who was thwarting his basic wish to solve it, he may have become enraged at the Riemann itself. The Riemann would have been the object of his thwarted wish, and rather than knowing it consciously, he would have repressed a great magnitude of rage toward the Riemann. The index of this magnitude of rage would most likely be determined by the same magnitude of his megalomania. This is because at the core of the megalomania, is the megalomaniacal wish, a wish of maximum intensity, perhaps equivalent to the wish for life itself. Thus, in the face of the thwarting of this wish, the rage would necessarily have had to have been atomic. This rage would have been enormous enough to create an implosion, so much so that he would have been left with rage-debris spanning, covering, and penetrating his psyche, equivalent to a permeating, pervasive radioactive contamination.

This then, could have been the basis of his schizophrenic meltdown. All of his schizophrenic symptoms, therefore, would be derivatives of this basic conflict; namely, love of the Riemann, and simultaneously, hatred of it. Expecting to solve the Riemann and thus confirm his grandiosity, and the actual failure to solve it, and an equally deflating blow to his megalomania. All of it created an ingenious way of both erasing and solving the Riemann simultaneously, albeit through a schizophrenic distortion.

Part of Nash's schizophrenic amalgam of distortions and hallucinations, included anti-Semitic sentiments. Here, it could also be hypothesized that, along with his other symptoms, all of which served the purpose of managing his megalomaniacal fury regarding his real failure to solve the Riemann, his anti-Semitic rantings were defensive machinations designed to isolate and nullify any credence given to Jewish genius. This speculation is based upon his experiences as a mathematician, often encountering Jewish scientists whom, he knew, were brilliant. In addition, Nash also occupied a place at Princeton, and despite his admiration of Einstein, in no way could he not have been envious of Einstein's stature in the world, certainly in popular culture, as the greatest genius of all. In this sense, the way Nash could eliminate any possible challenge to his own megalomaniacal assumption as being the greatest of all, would be to necessarily nullify Jews generally and Jewish scientists in particular. It is proposed that if not for this schizophrenic megalomaniacal state of failure regarding the Riemann, Nash's focus would be on his work, and his relationship with Jewish friends or colleagues may not have had the slightest tinge of anti-Jewish feeling whatsoever. Perhaps the only issue was his conviction that if any scientist was going to solve the Riemann, the likelihood was that that scientist would be a Jew; a Jewish scientist, genius, of whom he knew many. To Nash, someone other than himself solving the Riemann was probably equivalent to psychological or emotional death. Since he may have believed that a Jewish scientist was the one likely to do it, then Jews were generally no good – to be negated.

Of course, before the onset of his schizophrenia, and despite his Asperger state, he still lived within, at least the minimal limits of normalcy. He had a family. In this respect, despite his Asperger condition, he made some attempt to care for a number of people. Nevertheless, it could be that in his personal, subjective sense of self-importance, his narcissism and megalomania called him to the Riemann, and it very well may have been that this focus prevailed as the defining circumstance of his adult life.

In addition to these speculations, it could be that there was another person, probably a mathematician, who could also qualify as a support person with respect to who could have been the original focus of Nash's anger – the human *who*. If this is so, such a person would have had to play an important role in Nash's emotional life around the time of his slide into greater pathology.

Treatment

In the treatment of this complex person, Professor John Forbes Nash, Jr., involving Asperger's imperatives and a schizophrenic overlay, it is possible that the schizophrenia may, in effect, be urged to a point of remission, or at the very least, be neutralized. This is a clinical possibility based upon the assumption that Nash's schizophrenia, despite the fact that his son, John Charles, was also schizophrenic, could be a functional impairment brought on by emotional pressures, and necessarily by the appearance of some epigenetic pathology awaiting its developmental time and pivotal circumstance, to reveal itself.

The same cannot be said of his presumed Asperger's condition. The Asperger's complex would have had to have clearly been with him from birth. In any therapy treatment, Nash would have to begin to see the connections between his narcissistic megalomaniacal great-man inner Asperger's tyranny, and how it would not permit his tyrannical self to be a lenient inner self. Rather, this tyrannical Asperger's inner self which may have needed to have him be the greatest of all, would have mercilessly pushed him to render his most ingenious solution to any problem he ever tackled. In Nash's case, this attempt at an ingenious solution may have been to repress his rage toward the Riemann and then to develop a schizophrenia in which each and every symptom of this pathology reflected part of a strategy he unconsciously used: (1) to think of himself as prevailing over the Riemann, and when that was not enough; (2) to try to renounce his American citizenship as an unconscious way of freeing himself from the perhaps tyrannical mandate of solving the Riemann. These circumstances may have been his only way to loosen the grip of this inner psychic tyranny. The schizophrenia also may have been a way to undermine the genetic tyranny of his presumed Asperger imperatives.

Thus, Nash would need to get in touch with his anger, this proposed rage regarding his assumed thwarted wish. Further, it is proposed that then the very life, the very essence of his schizophrenia, would be challenged. The axiom remains: *Where there is no repressed anger, not only will there not be a symptom, there **cannot** be a symptom.*

The therapeutic objective with Nash, therefore, would be to implement the symptom-code presented here, including explication of the *wish*, the *repressed anger*, and the *who*, and then to penetrate the assumed meaning of his schizophrenia. Given his true genius, he is most likely, and happily, a prisoner of the ingenuity of connections and phenomena, his own included, that would be able to be explained to him, and certainly, without a doubt, understood by him. It is probably also true that he would have no choice but to be compelled by any powerful theoretical organization. The point is, that a man of Nash's scientific brilliance and intuitive powers, might be stronger than the schizophrenic Nash, with his morbid compensatory strategy of dealing with his Riemann demon.

Thus, given Nash's beautiful mind, when faced with truth, and the powerful beauty of truth – that is, being compelled by consciousness, in seeing the seductions, powers, and tricks of the unconscious, he may, under such irresistible thinking circumstances, then be subject to relinquishing his citizenship in the country of schizophrenic pathology. Any remaining pathology would be a form of resistance to knowing. In psychoanalytic parlance, resistance is merely a fortification of repression. Even his auditory hallucinations are meaningful with respect to reflecting his presumed original basic repressed wish, to solve the Riemann. Thus, the therapeutic treatment task would be to: (1) help Nash lift this repression; (2) understand the wish; (3)see that the repression is a repression of rage; and, (4) at the very least, identify the Riemann as the very possible personified *who*.

The final piece in the application of the symptom-code would be for Nash to implement a *doing* thing related to the original problem, presumed here to be possibly his attempt to solve the biggest problems such as the revision of quantum theory, but more likely, his desire to solve the Riemann Hypothesis. What this *doing* thing could be, would have to be worked out with Nash himself. An interesting prospect, indeed, considering of course, that given Nash's brilliance, it could possibly be that it will be Nash himsel that figures out what this *doing* thing could be.

Conclusion

True, this entire chapter is highly speculative, a metapsychological study. Nevertheless, the theoretical synthesis seems large enough to include virtually each and every symptom of Nash's pathology, and possible pivotal variables have been identified as likely culprits in the process of Nash's decline into a bizarre life.

The symptom-code of the *wish, repressed anger*, the *who*, and a *doing* thing related to the original problem, offered here as a template to understand and organize most, and possibly all of the phenomena of Nash's decline into pathology, has been one way to take a great amount of anecdotal material, and a complex set of pathological symptoms, and organize them into what might be an understandable model that possibly could be utilized in a therapeutic framework, even with Professor John Forbes Nash, Jr., this genius – a man with a beautiful Asperger's mind.

Part IV
Examining Theoretical Issues of the Symptom-Code

Chapter 21
Acting Out: The First Symptom, and the Primacy of Anger or Sex

In Part IV, a number of theoretical issues will be raised that are directed at a critical examination of various questions regarding the efficacy of the symptom-code as a cure-all for a certain class of symptoms. Most of these symptoms were those of recent onset, and which had not fully contaminated the personality. Thus, the person and the symptom remained distinguishable, and such symptoms were seen to be encapsulated in a neurotic and nonpsychotic state. This class of symptoms was also not encrusted in a chronic somatized transformation, and in addition was free from any neurological or biological influences. In other words, these curable symptoms, for the most part, were those that remained in an ego-alien position in relation to the personality.

Of course, this formulation of the difference between accessible curable symptoms and the more inaccessible resistant symptoms, raises many questions. We need to ask, for example, what it is about a symptom, in the context of a psychosis, or what it is about a symptom that has been chronically somatized, or what it is about a symptom that has been sustained for a lifetime, which makes it relatively immune to psychotherapy using the proposed symptom-code, or for that matter, using any psychotherapy method at all?

There are many such issues to examine, along with questioning the basic axioms that have been presented. After all, an axiom is also an uncontested assumption. We need to contest the assumptions made, and examine the probability of their so-called self- evident truths.

Is it Anger or Sex?

An indirect approach to understanding whether it is anger or sex that constitutes the basic emotion, impulse, or instinct involved in symptom formation, can be examined in light of the following question: In prehistoric man, what was the first symptom? If we go back in time, 50,000 or even 75,000 years ago to the early Pleistocene Era, to *Australopithecus prometheus*, could we speculate as to whether such a being had psychological symptoms? And if so, what might the first one have been? And further, would such a symptom be any different from what we see in modern man? Of course, would this symptom have been the same for Java man of the Pithecanthropine or *Homo erectus* species, of the middle Pleistocene Era, or Cro-Magnon man of the *Homo sapiens* species, approaching the late Pleistocene Era, even 30,000 years ago?

One way to understand what this first symptom may have looked like, is to examine the axiom or the symptom-code element concerned with the management of anger. This axiom of the symptom-code states: *Where there is repressed anger, not only will there be a symptom, there **must** be a symptom.* This axiom is invoked when a person's wish is blocked or thwarted. With the thwarted wish, at once there is created the feeling of helplessness or disempowerment; that is, wishes that are gratified are empowering, and in contrast, wishes that are thwarted, are disempowering. Since an accepted premise or hard core psychological law holds that all helplessness breeds rage, then it certainly seems that in a state of even momentary disempowerment, the evolutionary impulse, or reflex, is to become angry. The answer to the question of why is this so is that when one is in a state of helplessness or disempowerment, then frequently, the only way to become reempowered, is to be angry. Anger is a release, an expostulation of power. It may not always be productive, or even successful in actually achieving reempowerment, and yet in that momentary state of helplessness, the release of anger brings relief in the sense of the feeling of reempowerment.

Seen from this perspective of empowerment versus disempowerment, it seems evident that anger, as an explosive expression of energy and power, could always be experienced as an empowerment. The same, of course, could not be said of a sexual impulse, which on the face of it is quite an iffy, and at best, conditional response to circumstances of disempowerment. In fact, there is probably a very high inverse correlation between an intense sexual impulse and an intense circumstance of disempowerment. However, the anger response to disempowerment certainly seems, even on the face of it, and with respect to each and every person, everywhere in the world, to be the ubiquitous response to all disempowerment.

The Primacy of Anger

Thus, in human affairs a picture of the primacy of anger begins to develop, especially when contrasted with the role of sexuality. The point is that we are all wish-soaked creatures and wishes want gratification. These wishes of ours are also not often ranked as to importance. Major and minor wishes are treated in much the same way. Everything is major when the wish is wished for. In a moment to moment discrete existential sense, and in terms of priorities of the psyche, individuals typically behave as though there may be no such thing as a minor wish. By and large, however, even though people do indeed make some distinctions between major and minor wishes, it would seem that the initial predilection is to respond in a large way, to any thwarted wish.

The issue is whether, when some wishes are thwarted, and anger invoked, is the anger then consciously retained and addressed, or is it instantly repressed, even before the person is aware of its existence? If repressed, then it is proposed that a symptom will begin to gestate, and the symptom will in turn presumably reflect a gratification of the original wish, albeit in a transformed, neurotic, or perverse form–the symptom. The symptom, therefore, will be the wish gratified, a Freudian discovery of major significance. And the symptom can include anything from the development of anxiety to a more generalized symptom of acting out.

In prehistoric man, anxiety would be the probable initial response to some real or perceived threat, but the sense of disempowerment resulting from a persistent feeling of danger or threat would surely have led to a chain of events, the likely purpose of which was to generate reempowering behavior despite the obvious protective, guarded, and fear behaviors that surely existed. Further, in prehistoric man, in the face of the existence of varieties of predators, as well as the experience of the greater force of nature, initial anxiety would necessarily have needed to be replaced by some motoric act in order to achieve some ambulatory possibility–some *doing* thing. Again, the aim of this *doing* thing would be to guard and secure the self – an attempt at mastery and therefore also reempowerment.

Thus, with respect to a generalized acting out, or even in a more undifferentiated expression of a symptom, it is proposed that in prehistoric man, for example, the first symptom may have been an undifferentiated one – generalized anxiety transformed to a generalized acting out, based upon the repression of anger regarding a thwarted wish, which would have been what it always has been, a wish to be empowered; fear leading to disempowerment, leading to anger, leading to repression of anger, leading to acting out.

The Psychoanalytic Understanding of Acting Out

In contrast to the psychoanalytic understanding of acting out, the psychiatric definition is satisfied by the identification of the person's inappropriate behavior; that is, a person's behavior constitutes the sine qua non of such a psychiatric definition. The psychoanalytic definition of acting out, however, revolves around the ubiquitous defense of *repression*, fortified especially in therapy sessions, by an ever present *resistance* to the treatment.

Thus, in psychoanalysis, acting out is seen as an attempt *not to know something* (via repression) by invoking *doing* (acting out) behavior. The process of not-knowing is accomplished through the use of repression. Therefore, when anger is repressed, the not-knowing is achieved by keeping the person out of touch with this self-same anger. In the most general undifferentiated sense, whatever symptom appears thereafter is an example of acting out; that is, *doing,* instead of knowing, the classic psychoanalytic understanding of acting out.

It would seem from this concatenation, that even in prehistoric man, the first symptom process must have been a morphing of initial anxiety and fear, generating endless disempowerments, and then to generalized acting out of anger. And the acting out, as stated, would have been based upon the repression of such anger. In prehistoric man, repression of anger was, at times, most likely the only choice. In all likelihood, acting out became the expression of a psychic equation, that is, the acting out was in symbolic form, an attempt to gain the wish, to gratify it. As man evolved, symptoms became gradually more specific, more differentiated, until a profusion of adaptive possibilities emerged in the form of psychological/emotional symptoms–from phobias to panic attacks, from obsessions and compulsions to somatized symptoms, and from delusions and hallucinations to any number of intrusive thoughts or even any number of psychotic regressive behaviors.

Thus, in this probabilistic theoretical examination of the management of anger, the repression of anger, the nature of acting out, the experience of anxiety, the relation of the wish to anger-repression, the nature of the symbolic equation of the symptom to the wish, the psychology of empowerment and disempowerment, as well as attempting to derive some clue as to the nature of symptoms from the dawn of human evolution, from all of this it seems that it is anger and not sex, that is the linchpin of symptom formation.

Abridging Traditional Psychoanalytic Understanding of Symptom Formation

In the conventional understanding of symptom development, the ego is in the driver's seat insofar as it is felt that the ego has to be strong and resilient enough to control the drives. These drives are considered to be id impulses. In conventional psychoanalytic theory, when symptoms appear, it is the drives that become implicated insofar as a conflict then develops between the ego, the control, and the id, the impulses. This conflict is then theorized as really being a compromise between the derivative of the drive on the one hand, and the fear regarding a sense of danger that emerges with respect to the breakthrough of the drives, on the other. In psychoanalytic theory, this compromise is formulated as the symptom.

Thus, in psychoanalytic understanding of the drives, these id impulses are thought of as both aggressive and sexual, implying always that either or both are responsible for generating symptoms. In the symptom-code presented in this volume however, and in the associated conceptualization of the nature of symptoms, this psychoanalytic traditional understanding of symptom formation would seem to need amending.

The challenge offered by the conceptualization of the present symptom-code and its underlying principles and axioms, would strongly argue only for anger as the derivative of the drive implicated in symptom formation. Of course, there can be sexual wishes that are thwarted, but that does not mean that it is the sexual repression, suppression, or frustration that is causing the symptom. When a sexual wish has been thwarted, like any thwarted wish, disempowerment or helplessness results, and it is this helplessness or disempowerment that will generate instant anger, conscious or not. It is this anger that when repressed, will generate the symptom. Again, a frustration of a sexual wish produces the same anger as does a frustration of a nonsexual wish, or any wish, for that matter. It is the anger, in response to thwarted wishes, that is ubiquitous in the formation of symptoms, not the sex.

In fact, it is proposed here, that *never* is the sexual impulse directly responsible for the formation of a psychological symptom. Only the repression of anger, and no other emotion, impulse, or drive, is responsible for the formation of symptoms. It is anger that is the linchpin because it is anger that is always invoked to manage the thwarting of wishes. The answer is not whether it is sex or anger that constitutes the key to the symptom process. The key to the symptom process only involves whether the anger is repressed producing a symptom, or not (producing no symptom). Now the axiom is formed: *If the anger is not repressed there will be no symptom. If the anger is repressed, not only will there be a symptom, but there* ***must*** *be a symptom.*

Despite this insistence on the primacy of anger and the pointed irrelevance of the sexual drive to the actual mechanics of symptom formation, nevertheless in the psychoanalysis of any patient, all sorts of historical analyses based on psychosexual stage considerations, as well as considerations of intrapsychic conflict, certainly still obtain, and these remain requisites in the understanding of the entire picture contributing to the analytic working-out and working-through process. If there is any emendation to be made, it is only with reference to clarifying what goes into the mechanics of symptom formation, and that is anger, not sex.

Illustrations with Clinical Vignettes

Brenner (1974), in contrast, offers examples of how sometimes it is the sexual implication that forms the symptom. He presents a clinical vignette of a mature woman who developed a symptom of vomiting. The interpretation given essentially accounts for the symptom as a reactivation of the woman's historical wish, during her early oedipal years, to be impregnated by her father. Her father's remarriage in the period of the woman's then adult life, ostensibly caused the vomiting symptom. By vomiting, she would deny her father's new marital situation and its sexual implication. By vomiting, she was essentially saying, "See, I'm vomiting. I have morning sickness." Hence, it is concluded that the woman used the vomiting symptom to gratify the original wish, in symbolic symptom form to have been impregnated by her father.

This is all well and good – but does it reflect a true dynamic? It could be that a different but related scenario is actually closer to what happened. For example, the woman could have resented that her father remarried for any number of reasons, even, or perhaps especially, for the reason regarding her reputed historical wish to be impregnated by him. Yet, it is more likely that she then repressed her anger about her father's new marriage, either because of abandonment feelings or because of the threat of losing her historical wish, or because a conscious objection would be embarrassing, or whatever. The important point is not that she repressed her sexuality, but that she repressed her anger about her father's marriage, or even about her ostensible unrequited sexual wish. In any event, because she very likely would have been angry about his marriage, then anger and not sexuality would be the key emotion that became subject to repression

Her father was the *who*, who was making her angry by his behavior – he married. Her wish was to keep him unmarried, so she began to vomit. The vomiting was more likely an attempt to expel, to rid herself of this new formation, this marriage. Of course, since the wish was an indirect avoidant one (for him not to marry), then it would be predicted that her symptom would be unpleasant and not pleasurable. Vomiting is not pleasurable.

Thus, in this case, her statement, "See I have morning sickness," as a message of the symbolic gratification of her wish may indeed be an accurate reflection of the correlation of the wish and the symptom. Nevertheless, to consider this connection to be a possible result of some sexual repression would, at best be tangential, and at worst be wrong, a tortured explanation and an incorrect explanatory stretch, at best. It is the repression of anger regarding the thwarting of her basic wish with respect to the *who*, her father, which reveals the mechanics in the birth of her vomiting symptom. It is this equation of the repressed anger to the *who*, that connects her wish to the symptom–and, it is proposed here, nothing else.

In another vignette (Brenner, 1974), a soldier developed an anxiety attack while on the front lines, and had to be removed from battle. This case also exemplifies how the repression of anger generates the symptom. The soldier's anxiety attack would be considered to be merely a symptom of the wish to flee the front line of danger. Parenthetically, anxiety attacks as symptoms would be always considered a result of repressed anger to some condition of helplessness. These sorts of attacks would be defined as fears or panics only on a manifest, concrete level. The soldier's helplessness or powerlessness presumably developed out of a sense of vulnerability on the front lines. Yet, most certainly, such helplessness always generates anger that then, because of the appearance of the anxiety attack necessarily implies that the soldier's anger was repressed. Without the repression, the anxiety-attack could not have crystallized, because, according to the understanding considered here, in the absence of repressed anger, there cannot be a symptom, including an anxiety attack.

With the repression of anger, anxiety emerges as a gratification of the wish to be protected. The anxiety above, is here seen as radiating from the repressed anger below, thereby satisfying the wish to escape danger. Since each basic emotion such as fear or anxiety contains its own fundamental nature, then when one is anxious or fearful, fleeing is the only wish that expresses the unidimensional nature of that particular emotion. Thus, in the case of the soldier, repressed anger produced an anxiety condition that then enabled the person to become removed from the perceived threat – wish gratified.

And this entire issue reveals a profound psychoanalytic implication that seems to invite, or strongly suggests, a revision of the Freudian understanding of symptom formation. The revision is expressed in the symptom-code; that is, the thwarted wish produces a sense of powerlessness that generates anger as a method of reempowerment. This anger when becoming instantly repressed, in turn, generates a symptom that is a perverse or neurotic way of gratifying the original wish. And this process does not depend on which psychosexual stage the original historical material was based, on how strong or weak was the ego, or how strong or weak was the id impulse. In this revision, the only factor that symptom formation seems to depend upon, is whether or not anger is repressed – and always in relation to a *who*.

If the anger is indeed repressed, the result will necessarily be an acting out (or acting-in), in the form of the development of a symptom. Since, it is proposed that general hostile acting out may likely have been the first symptom of human history, then it may be possible to trace this dimension of hostility to the present, where rather than exhibiting generalized hostility, evolutionary development has enabled such acting out to crystallize in the form of the appearance of a matrix or gradient of differentiated symptoms; in the case of the soldier, an anxiety symptom. This gradient of differentiated symptoms is now in such profusion that to be parsimonious in understanding them entire categories of symptoms have been conceived. These include phobias, obsessions, compulsions, intrusive thoughts, and so forth, as well as more overarching distinctions presented here – namely accessible and inaccessible symptoms.

Summary

In this chapter, the repression of anger was examined and said to be the linchpin of all psychological symptomatology. Further, with respect to the mechanics of symptom formation, a proposed revision of traditional psychoanalytic understanding of symptoms and their formation was suggested, in which, from the point of view of curing symptoms, considerations of psychosexual historical material and sexual impulses were relegated to a secondary position, although sustained in importance with respect to the psychoanalytic treatment process. In contrast, from the point of view of the mechanics of symptom formation, as well as the cure of symptoms, anger and its repression, in relation to the wish and the *who*–the object–were elevated as the basic and sole variables accounting for such symptom phenomena.

In the following chapter, the difference between symptoms that can be cured by the talking method and through the use of the symptom-code will be discussed, in contrast to those symptoms that resist such treatment and seemingly nullify the effectiveness of the symptom-code. The issue of what makes this difference will be considered.

Chapter 22
Symptoms Versus Character Traits: Accessible Versus Inaccessible Symptoms

It has been proposed in this volume that, with respect to psychotherapy treatment, symptoms can be classified as either accessible or inaccessible. What this essentially means is that there are some symptoms (the inaccessible symptoms), that resist cure through psychotherapy, while other symptoms (the accessible symptoms), that indeed, can be cured through psychotherapy.

Further, it has been proposed that those intractable inaccessible symptoms, those that are not responsive to the power of the symptom-code, actually join the patient's repertoire of character traits, and in effect, those symptoms then operate in the personality as though they were character traits. Assuming the truth of this ostensible and proposed phenomenon, then of course, application of the symptom-code to these inaccessible symptoms would not, strictly speaking, be addressing a symptom. It would be as if one were treating a malady that started out as a common cold but developed into a sinus infection, thereby perhaps and in all likelihood, requiring a different order of treatment.

It is proposed that there are symptoms that start out as symptoms, but are then subject to the vicissitudes of some yet unknown process or phenomenon of the psyche, so that the symptom becomes translated into a character trait, or becomes integrated into the character structure and then behaves as a trait, or is knitted into the character structure, as it were, minus any ego-alien tension regarding its presence. Under this sort of condition, such a symptom presumably loses its symptom context insofar as it no longer addresses issues solely regarding satisfaction of the wish. Rather, it is proposed, the symptom remains as an idiosyncratic symptom presence, but assumes another hue within the personality – that of a trait.

Therefore, it misses the point to treat such a symptom with psychotherapy that targets cause and effect relationships, ties the symptom to the memory of a repressed emotion in relation to an object, a person. Thus, applying the symptom-code to such a translated symptom, no less a code that uses the same metapsychological notion of direct cause and effect between the repressed emotion and the object, is also to miss the point. In contrast, to treat a symptom that has been converted into a trait would all be well and good provided that the symptom as character trait could be reconstituted as, strictly speaking, a symptom. Then, psychotherapy and the application of the symptom-code could be a powerful tool in helping the patient to more efficiently cure the symptom. But treating an intractable symptom in this way, as though it exists within a typical symptom context, is perhaps a failure to understand that: (1) the symptom is no longer merely a symptom; (2) there needs to be a clear understanding of the difference between symptom and character trait; (3) the symptom in the psyche has been converted into a character trait and needs to be reconstituted as, strictly speaking, a symptom, and only then treated as a symptom; and, (4) the treatment then should consider targeting the psychology of character trait structure, in addition to that of symptom structure.

What, Why, Who, When, Where, and How What Happens?

What Happens?

The question is, What happens to the symptom that transforms it into a character trait? The answer is a tentative one based entirely on theoretical guesses, educated though they may be. The important point seems to be that it is probably the case that when the anger is repressed (and repressed toward the *who*, that is, with respect to the *memory* of the *who*) then the symptom remains a symptom, and would be definitely subject to the application of the symptom-code as it can be utilized in the therapy. However, the assumption is now made that in the psyche unconscious forces operate in a number of ways so that it is possible, under certain circumstances, for the memory of the *who*, to be detached or delinked from the repression of the anger. In such a scenario, the anger remains repressed without a *who* toward whom this anger was originally attached. The memory of the *who* is now shifted away from the repressed anger and this anger is left perhaps aimless, having no memory of an object.

It should be remembered that one of the axioms upon which the symptom-code is based concerns one of the immutable laws of emotion; that is, that an emotion is only realized as an emotion when it takes an object. What this means is that the emotion (in this case, anger that is repressed), is only completed as an emotion when it attaches to its intended person, its object. In this way, as a result of the attachment to a new object, the repressed anger can then fulfill its role – be an emotion.

However, this search becomes perseverative because when the memory of the *who* becomes detached from the repressed anger, and therefore, the nature of the symptom becomes altered, then this search for the object is unproductive because the goal can never be met; the goal being a discovery and reattachment of the memory of the original object to the repressed anger. Yet, if only to feel satisfied, this tropistic search continues. In such a scenario, because the memory of the original object is erased, then the model for any true transference figure to exist, is also just about entirely absent. It would be an emotion trying to complete itself but not knowing why or even how.

This endless search of a *who* by the repressed anger, means that such a symptom will resist all attempts to be reached. The symptom becomes a moving target, all of its energy being consumed by this never-ending search for something, perhaps the true *who*. Instead, the question becomes: Does finding a surrogate *who* (a transferential figure or figures) ever satisfy the emotion (the anger) in any real sense? This is what may determine why the symptom becomes intractable, inaccessible. It is a generalized repetition compulsion acted out by mechanisms of the psyche that produce perseverative psychological impulses. The need such mechanisms serve concerns attempts to master the original problem of reigniting the memory, reattaching the object to the repressed anger. Thus, it would seem that when the repressed anger remains attached to its target object, the *who*, then the symptom is retained in the psyche as an encapsulated one. In such a case, the symptom is not part of the person's character trait context, but rather remains within the domain of the psyche concerned with wishes. In this sense then, the symptom that remains apart from the character trait context would be considered the class of symptom accessible to psychotherapy and indeed, could be cured by applying the symptom-code.

Why Does it Happen?

As stated above when, in the psyche the *who* or the memory of the *who* becomes detached from the repressed anger, then this anger remains without an object. This may mean that the emotion, the anger, will need to find another object with whom to bond or become attached. The basic question, however, is: Why does the memory of the *who* detach from the anger? The answer could possibly involve the infrastructure of the anger itself, as in a cumulative sense it impacts the psyche. Simply put, the anger can be overpowering with respect to the integrity or viability of the psyche. In its pure repressed form that fuels the stasis of the symptom, the anger may become too much for the psyche to handle. This kind of anger then, may threaten the very cohesion of the psyche so that under such a condition, an immediate imperative of the psyche would dictate the evocation of a process to relieve this sort of threat to its existence. And of course, such a threat can also result when one's ego is configured with a so-called, *thin stimulus-barrier*. What this means is that there are individuals who are not resilient enough to withstand the intensity of certain emotions – especially anger, or its higher intensity of fury or rage. And this sort of less than resilient ego does not necessarily imply the thin stimulus-barrier of the borderline diagnosis, primarily because borderline reactions are usually characterized by episodic eruptions of anger, rather than by episodic repressions of anger.

Thus, to answer the question of *why* the symptom transforms into a trait, an analysis of the structure, valences, and nature of each particular anger needs to be identified, even enumerated, and of course, analyzed. It is here proposed that in a basic sense these constituents of the anger would include the factors of magnitude, intensity, depth, and duration of the anger. In concert, and at high levels of activation, these factors of magnitude, intensity, depth, and duration of the anger, will most likely create the signal for the psyche to begin the process of transporting the symptom out of the domain in the psyche devoted to the gratification of wishes, and into the domain or realm in the psyche of character trait structure.

It is the magnitude, intensity, depth, and duration of the anger that needs to be examined in order to understand why the memory of the *who* detaches from the anger. These seem to be the essential factors of the anger, its infrastructure, that give it its final form.

Magnitude of the Anger

In examining the anger, it could be asked: What was the magnitude of this anger?; that is, how much of the psyche did it cover, or radiate? All of it? Most of it? Some of it? Hardly any of it?

Given an intact ego, the point is that the more of the psyche this anger affects or radiates, the greater the possibility that the connection of the memory of the *who*, will be severed from the repressed anger. The corollary is also a possibility; that is, the less radiated the psyche is by such anger, the less probability there may be of a disconnection between the memory of the *who* and the repressed anger.

Intensity of the Anger

How shrill is the anger? How intense was it? How dense was its implosive power? Another piece to the puzzle of what happens to cause the memory of the *who* to become detached from the repressed anger is thus offered a companion factor. If the implosive power of the anger was great, then the probability increases that the disconnection between the memory of the *who* and the anger, increases. But if the implosive power of the anger was not great, then the probability of the connection between the memory of the *who* and anger, more likely would be sustained.

Of course, were the *magnitude* of the anger to have permeated all or most of the psyche, and along with this, the *intensity* or implosive power of the anger also was great, then the probability of the detachment between the repressed anger and the memory of the *who* would be predictably increased.

Depth of the Anger

How deep is the anger, how far does it penetrate to the core of the psyche? It would be predicted that the deeper it goes, the greater is the possibility that the memory of the *who* will be disconnected from the repressed anger. In this sense, such a disconnection would then contribute to the greater inaccessibility of the symptom to normal psychotherapy through the use of the symptom-code. Of course, the resilience of a person's ego now also comes into play. With a stronger ego, even intense anger could have a more difficult time penetrating deeply into the psyche. In this sense, a better ego is a better shock absorber.

With a *magnitude* of anger covering most or all of the psyche, and with a great *intensity* in the implosive power of the anger, along with an extensive penetration of anger to the core of the psyche, reflecting either a maximum or near maximum *depth* of penetration, it would be predicted that the symptom would in all likelihood be even more predictably inaccessible to psychotherapy. This would be true because under these conditions of the vicissitudes and nature of the repressed anger, the vast probability is that, in the alliance of all of these infrastructural factors to the anger, the detachment of the memory of the *who* from the anger that is repressed, would be more definite.

Duration of the Anger

Finally, the fourth infrastructural dimension in the formation of a process that pries loose the memory of the *who* from the anger, or another significant factor that can contribute to such a detachment, and thereby promote the transport of the symptom from the psyche's domain of wishes into its realm of character traits, is the variable of *duration*. How long has it been since the patient began experiencing the symptom? At a certain point in its duration a symptom, rather than being considered an acute phenomenon, becomes a chronic one. It is this historical or temporal dimension that distinguishes between acute and chronic symptoms.

Along with *duration* of the anger, the variables of *magnitude, intensity*, and *depth*, as a full complement of variables, can cause a change in any critical threshold that ignites the need for the psyche to delink the memory of the *who* from the repressed anger, thereby evoking the migratory process that sends the symptom from the domain of wishes to the domain of traits. When such a critical threshold is not reached, the symptom would remain in a state that still may be treated by way of the symptom-code. This is in contrast to a symptom where the *magnitude, intensity, depth*, and *duration* of the repressed anger is great, thereby suggesting that the symptom has become inaccessible to therapy, and along with its symptom configuration has acquired membership in the character trait context.

These then, it is proposed, are the factors that distinguish between symptoms that are accessible to treatment with the symptom-code, and those that are not treatable with such a code. Rather, the inaccessible symptoms would require a character-code to cure, because basically, although they are still symptoms, they are no longer solely symptoms.

Thus, to treat this new form, a symptom that is visible as a symptom, but has become a trait, requires an understanding of the structure of character formation along with character defenses, and should not rely solely on an understanding of the formation of psychological/emotional symptoms proper.

Where Does it Happen?

Where does the symptom do its migrating from the domain of wishes to the domain of traits? The hypothesis is that *it happens in the psyche*, an abstraction. To visualize the psyche is to utilize whatever heuristic device that seems useful. This could be an amalgam of models, or even a single structural one. For example, the psyche can be seen structurally as an orb, or conceived as an amalgam of Freudian models such as intrapsychic, structural, topographical, psychosexual, genetic, adaptive, and economic, or as the mind-organ that coheres it all, personality, cognition, emotion, motivation, into some syndromal synthesis. Even in visualizing the psyche, it may be conceived that the psyche is constructed in at least three dimensions, and that within this scope of such a metaphysical arena are various domains of personality, including emotions, drives, wishes, defenses, cognition, motivation, attitudes, and so forth, all dynamically related and ultimately governed by psychoevolutionary and epigenetic structural rules. Whatever it is that happens, is considered here to happen in the psyche, this abstraction that lends itself to any number of visualizations and conceptualizations.

When Does it Happen?

If the transformation or shift of the symptom to the realm of character traits does take place, it would occur rather quickly, and over time would become integrated into the repertoire of character traits so that the symptom would become part of that person's personality print. "Rather quickly," does not necessarily mean instantly. The experience of the symptom, underpinned by repression of anger, and accompanied by a wish, would, always appear as a symptom and act like a symptom, no matter its location in the psyche. *When* the migration occurs, however, would depend upon the magnitude, intensity, depth, and duration of the anger. When these factors are great, then the psyche would possibly experience a "psyche-quake," so much so, that an implicit imperative regarding the survival of the psyche would, in all likelihood dictate, even mandate some process to deliver this symptom out of the domain of wishes in the psyche and into the fabric of the personality. Perhaps the only place the symptom would be able to go would be into the psyche's realm of character traits. This shift or transformation may become more and more cemented, based upon elapsed time. Thus, it happens during the accrued duration of time that elapses from the moment that the psyche experiences a challenge to its integrity, to the time of the process whereby the psyche expels the symptom, either by shifting it, transforming it, or both.

Who is the *Who*?

With respect to symptoms, the *who* is a reference to the object. Yet, there really are two *who's*. The standard *who* is the object of the patient's anger. It was this anger that could not be directly expressed to the object, and therefore needed to be repressed. When the anger is repressed, the object becomes the subject, and therefore, the anger attacks the self. In other words, the subject (the self) becomes the surrogate for the original intended object of the anger, the other person–the *who*. Thus, when the anger takes the self, in a way, then two *who's* exist.

How Does it All Happen?

Now that some theoretical attempt has been proposed with respect to the issue of the psyche protecting itself from threat and challenge to its integrity, especially with respect to the process that shifts the symptom to the domain of traits, the question arises as to how it all happens. How does the psyche enable the symptom to migrate out of the realm of wishes and into the realm of traits? One answer is perhaps revealed in the discussion above on the what, why, who, where, and when of the psyche. It has been proposed that the nature of the repressed anger can be the motivating ingredient that forces the psyche to maintain its equilibrium. Whenever tension becomes too much to handle, then the equilibrium of the psyche can be sustained probably only by the recalibration of the tension within its boundaries. However, when this presumed increase of psychic tension becomes threatening (perhaps a threat to the very existence of the person's psychological life in the form of the threatened viability and integrity of the psyche), then such tension becomes an urgent alarm signal. In this sense the psyche is the central salient agency of a person's psychological existence.

Thus the question is again raised. How does the psyche manage to get the symptom translated from the domain of wishes, to the domain of traits? It is assumed that the initial tension within the psyche that motivates this migration, results from the nature of the repressed anger. The memory of the *who* is detached from the anger because the magnitude, intensity, depth, and duration of the anger becomes too much for the psyche to handle. The migration takes place in the abstraction we identify as the psyche. It takes place when the anger becomes too large for the psyche to feel comfortable in its management.

At this point, when presumably the psyche experiences the need to extrude the symptom from the realm of wishes, it is possible that it does so by the use of defenses. Thus, it is proposed that *how* it happens is through the use of defense mechanisms; that is, defense mechanisms can be utilized to incubate this translation of symptoms in the psyche's domain of wishes into the psyche's realm of traits. Within the psyche's domain of wishes, the symptom remains an accessible one and can be efficiently addressed with the symptom-code in a process of cure through psychotherapy. When, however, the symptom is processed through the psyche, so that it ultimately metamorphoses at least into traitlike form (i.e., retaining also its symptomness) and into the realm of traits, then there are various specific defense mechanisms that can be recruited by the psyche to accomplish this process.

In the following chapter, these mechanism of defense will be delineated, and it will be proposed that there exists a certain class of defenses that permit such a transformation to take place, while other more usual defense mechanisms are not at all suited for this kind of shifting of domains in the metapsychological arena of the psyche.

Chapter 23
The Metamorphosis of Symptoms:
The Domain of Wishes
and the Domain of Traits

It is proposed, that in the psyche various mechanisms of defense are utilized in the transformation and shift of the symptom from the domain of wishes to the domain of character traits. Of course, psychoanalytically, all mechanisms of defense are conceived as operating within the dynamic rules of the psyche, and by the laws of the unconscious. Yet, in order to understand the hypothesized phenomenon of this shift of symptom from a wish dominated encapsulated neurotic state into a trait dominated character or characterological state, it would seem to be necessary to distinguish between two kinds or classes of defense.

In conventional psychoanalytic theory, the defense system, originally gestates with respect to the needs of the ego, and defenses are considered to be ego defenses. Yet, it could be argued that defenses are artifacts of a psychoevolutionary process in which the vicissitudes of basic emotions created imperatives for mechanisms to become active that could manage each of these emotions. In this sense, defenses could also be considered *emotion defenses*. For example, the defense of displacement could easily be understood as developing in evolution to manage the basic emotion of anger. Similarly, the defense of compensation could also be seen as having developed to address the issues of loss, inadequacy feelings, sorrow, or even depression. Compensatory behavior as a reaction to loss, for example, is an experience common to all people.

Further support to this idea of the birth and ontogony of defense as inextricably related to the needs of emotion, is perhaps revealed by the plasticity of the entire defense system; that is, the defense system as well as individual defenses, although perhaps developed to address the needs of specific emotions, are also very well adapted, so that particular defenses can be utilized to manage any other number of emotions, either as individual defenses or in defense clusters. For example, the management of obsessional states can enlist a cluster of defenses that include not only intellectualization, but also rationalization, sublimation, undoing, and isolation. This adaptational plasticity of the defense system can explain therefore, why in evolution, this system was highly selected (Kellerman, 1980; Plutchik, 1980).

Actually, considerable theoretical as well as empirical studies have been published with specific reference to this sort of understanding, as well as providing a general theoretical underpinning to the notion of defenses as emotion derived (Kellerman, 1979, 1980, 1983, 1987; Kellerman & Burry, 1997; Plutchik, 1980, 1994).

Also, any sole defense mechanism is called upon in its daily duty, to manage the basic structural constituents of emotion; that is, to manage the transitory nature of emotion. This transitory characteristic of emotion can be seen in the ebb and flow of everyday life where emotions are instantly experienced, are modified, changed, and frequently otherwise fleeting. It is also probably true that these typical emotion defenses, or as they are more typically referred to, as ego defenses—including repression, compensation, denial, displacement, intellectualization, isolation, projection, rationalization, regression, sublimation, undoing, and so forth–are also utilized in the fortification and cementing of character traits. An important point to note, however, is that such defenses are proposed as quite secondary in their use as significant factors in the formation of such character traits.

Rather than these so-called emotion defenses being essentially responsible for the formation and cementing of such character traits, another class of defense appears as actually the more corresponding mechanisms of these character-trait formations. This other class of defenses may be called character defenses, and are different in definition as well as function, than are the emotion defenses referred to above.

The character defenses have not developed to manage transitory states such as the basic emotions or even to manage more subtle mixed emotions. These character defenses are products of the psyche that synthesize the presumed compromises of instinctual drives with the demands of reality. The character defenses then, help to create establishments of reflexive, automatic patterns of behavior or traits, which when cemented as trait organizations, or trait clusters, or personality trait profiles, come to exist in more permanent arrangements, as more permanent etchings of the personality. These character defenses then, bind impulses and create each person's more permanent or consistent personality print.

The Class of Character Defenses

As emotion defenses (or ego defenses) manage emotion (mostly with respect to the *transitory* nature of emotion), character defenses, as stated, are utilized by the psyche to arrange, organize, and hold in place, more permanent fixtures of the personality–the traits. These character defenses therefore, are instrumental in the formation of enduring personality-trait patterns. This explication of character defenses as they stand in contrast to so-called emotion defenses, is examined further by Kellerman (1987), and Kellerman and Burry (1997).

The amalgam of character-defenses include:

Identification

This character defense is to character traits what repression is to emotion. Identification is a ubiquitous phenomenon that occurs axiomatically. It is the common underlying element in the development of trait patterns and acts to create reflexive, automatic, non-anxious behavior in the subject. Identification acts as a control over whatever configuration of personality finally forms.

Internalization

This character defense absorbs or infuses values and attitudes from model objects or figures, and imprints them so that such values and attitudes can ultimately prevail over the press of other external influences on the personality.

Splitting

This character defense enables self-contained compartmentalizations to exist in the psyche. Thus, splitting prevents the ambiguity that would ordinarily be associated with conflict. Individuals can be divided into good and bad objects, and idealizations as well as devaluations can be directed to the same person, rendering contradictions insignificant.

Turning Against the Self

This character defense enables hostility that is relatively intolerable, to shift from the object to the self. Thus, despite an increase of internal complexity, the subject is then able to more easily tolerate particular external conflict or pressures.

Symbolization

This character defense enables wishes, fantasies, and impulses, to become disguised through internal or external representations. Freud first indicated that it is the capacity for symbolization that largely determines, and underlies, the basis of character structure. Josephs (1992), elaborates and points out that Freud came to this conclusion by seeing that the essence of symbolization in the development of character traits concerns the notion of the unacceptable idea, impulse, emotion, or attitude, needing to find a place to reside. The answer was that the symbolic is connected to the unconscious because of the unacceptable idea. Actually, in conventional psychoanalytic understanding, symbolization permits an indirect or substitute satisfaction of the wishes. Freud regarded these wishes as unacceptable.

In the theoretical formulation proposed here, however, it is assumed that symbolization permits gratification of wishes to occur, but not merely with respect to unacceptable wishes. Rather, symbolization can indeed permit gratification of unacceptable as well as thwarted wishes which may not be unacceptable, but which may have become thwarted because of a possible variety of other reasons, all however, related to the connection of self-interest, survival, and fear.

The idea of symbolization is crucial to the understanding of several important seeming conundrums. For example, Freud's ingenious discovery that every symptom reflects and represents a particular wish in a completely gratified way, albeit in neurotic form, meant that the wish was symbolized in the symptom, and as the symptom. This insight also permitted Freud to understand that because the symptom represents the gratified wish, then everyone loves their symptoms (whether they know it or not), even those that are painful, because these symptoms are really the wishes, gratified.

The idea that character formation is in part, based on the capacity for symbolization, also has great currency in contributing to the understanding of why the wish joins the anger in repression. The symbol contains the essence of the wish and is sustained, fueled by the repressed anger. Also, when anger cannot be directly expressed to its intended object, it becomes instantly repressed, so much so, that the subject is not aware of the anger ever having even existed. Then, when the anger, alloyed with the wish is repressed, a symptom will necessarily appear. The rules governing such a connection between repressed anger and the appearance of a symptom are based on theoretical insights presented throughout this volume.

Parenthetically, such insights represent a clear departure from traditional Freudian understanding that a symptom is, strictly speaking, derived from some childhood sexual trauma and that because of the failure of repression in adult life, infantile sexual impulses find their release and end up causing symptoms. The departure here is based on the notion that symptoms only derive from repressed anger against a *who* someone who has thwarted a wish, and is not at all a function of some infantile sexual disturbance. In fact, it is proposed that the only way infantile sexuality can contribute to the formation of symptoms, concerns the thwarting of a sexual wish–at any time during development, including, but not necessarily solely during childhood–and because of this thwarting of the sexual wish, the subject (whether child or adult) becomes angry, and cannot, because of any number of factors (especially those factors of survival), express this anger directly to the object. Then, the anger, and not the sexuality, is repressed.

The Wish and the Anger

With respect to character formation and symbolization, it is still necessary to set forth how and why the wish joins the anger in the repression. The answer may be approached by examining how the anger "understands" what the thwarted wish was. Since the symptom reflects the thwarted wish, then this also may mean that the anger understood that the wish was thwarted, or, more importantly, what that wish was.

The question then arises, whether anger, as a basic drive or emotion with a presumed unidimensional personality (to attack) also, and perhaps surprisingly, has a cognitive component to its nature as well. Can the anger know something, in this case about the wish? According to Freud, the answer would not be in the affirmative. The answer would not be that the anger understands the wish as though some communicational interaction between them exists. Rather, it seems that a hard core Freudian proposition would predict that it is the symbolization of the wish that accompanies the anger, via repression, into the unconscious, and not that the anger is intelligent, above and beyond what is here considered its attack imperative, its basic nature.

Of course, a hypothesis can be entertained that suggests the possibility that perhaps the anger (or for that matter any other basic emotion) does in fact, possess cognitive capacity, especially, or even perhaps only, with respect to symbolization. That is, that perhaps anger, or any other basic emotion actually "understands" symbolization or "understands" the valence of the symbol as it represents wishes. This possibility raises some interesting implications regarding the psychology, and even perhaps, the morphology of basic emotions, in this case, anger. However, it seems far more likely that the psyche arranges for the possibility of the anger to be repressed, while simultaneously capturing the essence of the wish in symbolic form, and *attaching* it to the anger; that is, in its split-second repression, the psyche attaches in symbolic form, the message of the wish, to the anger. Thus, the anger and the essence of the wish are repressed together, and through the process of repression, as well as for the reason of the repression, become attached. They then coexist in the psyche's domain of wishes. In this sense, the basic emotion (in this case, anger), retains its unidimensionality. Therefore, the possibility of a cognitive capacity to basic emotions seems theoretically undermined.

In addition, when, in the unconscious, the anger, and the memory of the *who* also remain attached, they then form an alliance, ultimately with symbolization comprising the symptom that occupies the *wish* domain of the psyche, the realm in which neurotic symptoms exist. It is these symptoms that are subject to cure through the use of the symptom-code and via psychotherapy, presented in Part II of this volume, "Accessible Symptoms."

The Migration of Symptoms in the Psyche

The psyche's domain of *wishes* is not the same as the psyche's domain of traits. In the domain of traits, it is proposed that symptoms may be part of this trait domain or realm, but as such, they may not be composed of a memory of the *who*, as fused with or attached to the *repressed anger*. Traits are configurations formed out of the mechanisms of identification, internalization, splitting, turning against the self, and symbolization. These are unconscious mechanisms of the psyche and therefore memory of a *who* is anathema to this trait region of the psyche.

The key point in the shift or metamorphosis or migration of the symptom from the domain of wishes to that of traits, is the proposed phenomenon of the repressed anger becoming detached from the memory of the *who*. This proposed delinking then ostensibly permits a migration of the symptom out of the psyche's domain of wishes, and into the psyche's realm of traits. Under this new condition of the symptom having been transformed (migrated, or metamorphosed) to the realm of traits, the symptom's inner imperative is changed, so that no longer can it be cured through use of the symptom-code. Now, the symptom needs a new approach, a symptom/trait-code. And as is well known, treatment of character structure is far more complex and difficult than treatment of a neurotic symptom state. At least in the neurotic symptom state, anxiety acts as a signal and even motivator for change, and the symptom remains ego-alien and apart from the personality trait structure. With character problems, however, the symptom as a trait presumably suffers from an absence of the signal of anxiety acting to motivate or induce change.

Thus, as a symptom in the domain of wishes, the wish is gratified in perverse or neurotic form and therefore we love our symptoms. Yet, they cause us difficulty, anxiety, embarrassment, and so forth, so from a practical vantage point, we also hate them. However, when because of the separation of the memory of the *who* from the repressed anger, the symptom then migrates to the domain of traits and no longer acts with tension and anxiety about itself.

This discussion has been concerned with identifying a basic distinction between a neurotic symptom and a character trait, and has provided a tentative answer to possibly illuminate why some symptoms resist change while others can be cured quite efficiently. Of course, according to this view of treatment, those symptoms that resist change and are relatively inaccessible to cure, have become trait symptoms and in the psyche correspond to the realm of *traits*. In contrast, those symptoms that are deemed here to be accessible to cure, are those symptoms that reside in the psyche, in the realm of *wishes*.

Summary

In this volume, the theoretical framework of the traditional view of symptoms, and their formation and treatment has been contrasted with an alternative understanding. In this alternative understanding, accessible symptoms, those that, it is claimed, can be cured through the symptom-code that is presented, and via the psychotherapeutic method, have been contrasted with inaccessible ones, those symptoms that resist change and are thought to require a different code, one concerned with the penetration of character traits and character structure.

Furthermore, an important difference in the fundamental understanding of symptoms has been asserted. Rather than seeing infantile sexuality as the crux of the matter in symptom formation, the theory proposed here, points to the basic or nuclear factor of all symptom formation as a process beginning with a thwarted wish and ending with the symbolization of that wish as associated with repressed anger. This repressed anger is fused with the memory of the *who*–the person or object toward whom the anger was initially directed but toward whom it could not be expressed.

The salient psychoanalytic shift here is from sexuality to anger. Of course, both drives of sexuality and anger satisfy the pleasure principle. Both are empowering insofar as both satisfy needs. But whether sexuality becomes repressed, or whether it is really anger about thwarted sexuality or about any other thwarted wish that becomes repressed, is the essential issue.

The answer, although tentative, nevertheless seems to have profound implications in understanding a variety of issues within the arena of the psychoanalytic discussion. The core shift of focus is that it is anger and not sexuality that becomes repressed and therefore, that anger is the salient variable in symptom formation. Anger now becomes the focus. Repressed anger produces symptoms,

while the repression of sexuality in relation to symptoms, in this particular theoretical framework, is not very relevant. Thus, it cannot be the use of a symptom
code containing basic terms of repressed sexuality, identification of the *who*, and
consciousness of the wish, that will cure symptoms. Rather, *only* a code that utilizes terms of identification of the *who*, with consciousness of the *wish*, and most
importantly, with a focus on repression of anger toward the *who*, that can ever
cure the symptom.

Assuming the veracity of this challenge then the next step is the development
of a trait-code that can address those inaccessible symptoms that resist cure, that
because of the delinking of the memory of the *who*, with that of the repressed
anger, have become symptoms as traits, and therefore do not exhibit the typical
characteristics of neurotic symptoms. In contrast, the neurotic symptoms exist as
encapsulations set apart from the character structure and contain palpable signal
anxiety regarding the presence of such symptoms.

In the psychoanalysis of symptoms therefore: (1) *repressed anger*; (2) fused
with a memory of the *who* toward whom the original anger was directed; (3) in
conjunction with the symbolization of the *wish,* all reside in the domain of the
psyche devoted to wishes; and (4) together with a consequent addendum to the
symptom-code of a *doing* activity related to the original wish, comprise the symptom-code that enables the subject to move from a behind *The Line* withdrawal
state, to an in front of *The Line* "doing" state.

Thus, it has been proposed throughout this volume that these four factors in the
dynamic of the psyche, represent the essence of the symptom-code, which when
applied to the treatment of symptoms that exist in the psyche's domain of wishes,
can efficiently lead to the cure of the symptom.

Coda

A new, although related theme emerges in relation to the entire consideration of
symptom psychology. That is, that to further understand the genesis of symptoms,
it may just be that symptoms involve a cluster of concerns that combined, constitute a syndrome common to all people. This syndrome may be identified as one
containing thematic strands of separation anxiety, dependency, sorrow, depression,
abandonment, and loss. This syndrome may be labeled "attachment/separation."
Thus, it may be that every symptom has as its fundamental reason for being, something connected with the broad issue of attachment/separation. In other words,
with respect to psychoanalytic drive theory, the ubiquitous reflex of anger (in this
case with reference to feelings of disempowerment), is likely to be animated by an
epigenetic trigger. And this epigenetic trigger – this environmental stimulus that
ignites the process that ultimately leads to symptom formation, always may be
based upon an attachment/separation theme.

In a future evolution of the symptom-code addressing both accessible as well
as inaccessible symptoms, the theme of attachment/separation may contribute to
a general synthesis. The reader is invited to consider this proposition related to

the theme of attachment/separation with each symptom that has been presented in this volume.

Taken as a whole however, the symptom-code presented here has generated a system of propositions, assumptions, and axioms, that congeal an array of phenomena, sufficient perhaps, to qualify as a body of work, to this point identified as: *The Psychoanalysis of Symptoms.*

References

Alexander, F. (1950). *Psychosomatic medicine.* New York: W.W. Norton.

Arlow, J. (1969). Unconscious fantasy and disturbances of conscious experience. *Psychoanalytic Quarterly, 38,* 1–27.

Arlow, J. & Brenner, C. (1964). *Psychoanalytic concepts and the structural theory.* (pp. 11). New York: International Universities Press.

Brenner, C. (1973). *An elementary textbook of psychoanalysis.* (2nd edition). (pp. 189). Garden City, New York: Doubleday.

Deutsch, F. (Ed.). (1953). *The psychoanalytic concept in psychoanalysis.* New York: International Universities Press.

Engel, G., & Schmale, A. (1967). Psychoanalytic theory of somatic disorders: conversion specificity and the disease onset situation. *Journal of the American Psychoanalytic Association, 15,* 344–365.

Fenichel, O. (1945). *The psychoanalytic theory of neurosis.* New York: W.W. Norton.

Ferenczi. S. (1950). On transitory symptom construction during the analysis. In: S. Ferenczi, (Ed.). *Sex in psychoanalysis.* (pp. 164–180). (Original work published 1912).

Freud, S. (1952a). The interpretation of dreams. In T. Strachey (Ed. & Trans.), *The standard edition of the complete psychological works of Sigmund Freud. Vols. 4–5,* (pp. 51–65; 133–156). London: Hogarth Press. (Original work published 1900).

Freud, S. (1953b). Fragment of an analysis of a case of hysteria. In J. Strachey (Ed. & Trans.), *The standard edition of the complete psychological works of Sigmund Freud. Vol. 7,* (pp. 1–122). London: Hogarth Press. (Original work published 1905).

Freud, S. (1955). Analysis of a phobia in a five-year-old boy. In: J. Strachey, *(Ed. & Trans.), The standard edition of the complete psychological works of Sigmund Freud. Vol.10,* (pp.1–147). London: Hogarth Press. (Original work published 1909).

Freud, S. (1959). Inhibitions, symptoms, and anxiety. In: J. Strachey (Ed. & Trans.), *The standard edition of the complete psychological works of Sigmund Freud. Vol. 20,* (pp. 177–250). London: Hogarth Press. (Original work published 1926).

Freud, S. (1962). The neuro-psychoses of defence. In J. Strachey (Ed. & Trans.), *The standard edition of the complete psychological works of Sigmund Freud. Vol. 3,* (pp. 41–61). London: Hogarth Press. (Original work published 1894).

Goldstein, K. (1939). *The organism.* New York: American Books.

Greenacre, P. (1958). Toward an understanding of the physical nucleus of some defense reactions. *International Journal of Psychoanalysis, 39,* 69–76.

Josephs, L. (1992). *Character structure and the organization of the self.* New York: Columbia University Press.

Kellerman, H. (1979). *Group psychotherapy and personality: Intersecting structures.* New York: Grune & Stratton.

Kellerman, H. (1980). A structural model of emotion and personality: psychoanalytic and sociobiological implications. In R. Plutchik, & H. Kellerman (Eds.), *Emotion: theory, research, and experience: Vol 1. Theories of emotion.* (pp.349–384). New York: Academic Press.

Kellerman, H. (1983). An epigenetic theory of emotions in early development. In R. Plutchik, & H. Kellerman (Eds.), *Emotion: theory, research, and experience: Vol. 2. Emotions in early development.* (pp.315–349). New York: Academic Press.

Kellerman, H. (1987). Emotion and the organization of primary process. In R. Plutchik, & H. Kellerman (Eds.), *Emotion: theory, research, and experience: Vol. 5. Emotion, psychopathology, and psychotherapy.* (pp.89–113). New York: Academic Press.

Kellerman, H. (1990). Nightmares and the structure of personality. In H. Kellerman (Ed.), *The Nightmare: Psychological and biological foundations.* (pp. 273–354). New York: Columbia University Press.

Kellerman, H. & Burry, A. (1997). *Handbook of psychodiagnostic testing: Analysis of personality in the psychological report.* (3rd ed.). Boston: Allyn & Bacon.

Luborsky, L. (1964). A psychoanalytic research on momentary forgetting during free association. *Bulletin of the Philadelphia Association for Psychoanalysis, 14,* 119–137.

Luborsky, L. (1996). *The symptom-context method.* Washington, D.C.: American Psychological Association.

Nasar, S. (1998). *A beautiful mind.* New York: Simon & Schuster.

Plutchik, R. (1980). *Emotion: A psychoevolutionary synthesis.* New York: Harper & Row.

Plutchik, R. (1994). *The psychology and biology of emotion.* New York: Harper Collins.

Rangell, L. (1959). The nature of conversion. *Journal of the American Psychoanalytic Association, 7, 632–662.*

Seligman, M. (1975). *Helplessness: On depression, development, and death.* New York: Freeman.

Index

Printed in the United States
93231LV00003B/322-339/A

9 780387 722474